WOMB

Barnsley Libraries

P.S.2027

Return Date

22.8.12.

3 8059 30021809 8

ABOUT THE AUTHOR

The youngest of four sons, Jim Hutt was born in South Kirkby in 1939. His education began in the infants' department of Northfield School in 1944. In September 1947 he entered the junior department of Queen Elizabeth Grammar School, Wakefield. He remained at Q.E.G.S. until 1958. With his heart set on entering the teaching profession, he gained invaluable experience as a student teacher in Hemsworth and Upton. Then in 1959 he began his training at Borough Road, Isleworth, Middlesex, and completed it at the James Graham College in Leeds. He began work at Northfield in 1963 and remained there until illness forced his early retirement towards the end of 1992, after almost thirty years of service. During that time he taught a full range of subjects to children of nine to thirteen years, though his particular interests were English and History. He estimates that he has had a hand in the education of almost two thousand South Kirkby children.

He and his wife Sherilyn live in South Elmsall. Their two daughters Sharon and Julie both spent four years at Northfield. Sharon worked as a supervisor in the purchasing department of Sirdar Textile Manufacturers in Wakefield until her untimely death in 1992; Julie is a qualified civil engineer.

Since retirement much of Jim's time has been spent in reading, particularly Victorian literature, and in writing, where his current pursuits centre upon a study of surnames in the South Kirkby, South Elmsall and Pontefract district.

THE NORTHFIELD LOG

*The Story of a School
as revealed by its log book*

by

J.A. Hutt

With a Foreword by
Richard Attenborough
(The Lord Attenborough, C.B.E.)

BRIDGE PUBLICATIONS

PENISTONE · ENGLAND

Bridge Publications
2 Bridge Street, Penistone
Sheffield S30 6AJ

Copyright© James A. Hutt 1995

First Published 1995

All rights Reserved. No part of this publication
may be reproduced, stored in a retrieval system
or transmitted, in any form or by any means,
electronic, mechanical, photocopying,
recording, or otherwise, without the prior permission
of the Copyright owner

British Library Cataloguing in Publication Data

Hutt, J.A.
   Northfield Log : Story of a School as Revealed by Its
   Log Book
   I. Title
   373.236094281

   ISBN 0-947934-32-4
   ISBN 0-947934-31-6 (pbk)

Photoset 10½ on 12pt Times Roman by Bridge Publications
Printed and Bound in Great Britain by
Whitstable Litho Printers Ltd., Whitstable, Kent

Contents

Illustrations and Log Extracts
Foreword
Location of South Kirkby (Map)
Introduction
Acknowledgements
South Kirkby's Schools (Map)

1	Pre-History	1
2	South Kirkby Wesleyan Sunday School	5
3	A Brand-new School	17
4	'How to sustain interest . . .'	25
5	The Miners' Strike of 1912	33
6	The Great War	38
7	The 1920s: Period of Poverty	45
8	Between the Wars — From the School Log	55
9	The Second World War	69
10	Improving Northfield's Image	72
11	John Thomas Glover	87
12	Northfield Middle School	91
13	Reminiscences	103
14	A Community Undermined	111
15	The Future of Northfield	115
	Four Hundred Years of Educational Opinion	120
	Sir Alec Clegg	123
	Index	128

Illustrations and Log Extracts

Northfield Methodist Chapel	xiv
National School and Schoolchildren, c.1905	xiv
How the Edwardian teacher dressed	4
First page of Northfield Log, 29th September 1902	6
First H.M.I. Report, April 1903	14-16
Williamson's heating survey, 13 January 1913	24
South Kirkby, c.1914	31-2
South Kirkby Colliery	36
'Miners Wake Up!' — The 1912 Strike	37
H.M.I. Report, 1922	48-49
Two pages from the Punishment Book, 1927 & 1930	53-4
Two Northfield School Reports, 1929 & 1930	67-8
'Salute the Soldier' Week, 1944	71
Portrait of J.T. Glover, Headmaster 1959-77	84
May Day at Northfield, 1947	85
Northfield in the late 1950s	85
Fourth Year Group, 1963 and The Staff, 1965	86
Fourth Year Group, 1967 and J.T. Glover's Middle School Staff, 1971	89
Two views of Northfield, 1967	90
The Second Year, 1970-1971	102
The First Year, 1988	110
The Northfield Staff, 1988	113
Northfield Art Display, 1917	114
Sir Alec Clegg	127

Foreword

MY FATHER was born in Stapleford, in Middle England, and my mother a few miles away in Long Eaton. As my maternal grandfather, Samuel Clegg, was headmaster of the local school, and my father a junior member of his staff, both my parents were destined to be profoundly influenced by his innovative attitude towards education. So too, of course, was Alec Clegg, his youngest child and only son.

The Cleggs and the Attenboroughs considered education to be of prime importance; but they were also, without exception, passionate aficionados of the visual arts. Indeed, one of my earliest memories, aged 11, is of being taken by my father from Leicester, where he was Principal of the University College, to the National Gallery in London, to admire the newly acquired Seurat, *Une Baignade*.

Although Alec was, in fact, my uncle, he was always regarded by my brothers and myself as more of an elder sibling, since there were so few years between us. I was therefore sufficiently close to him to know what immense pleasure he must have derived from taking my father to Northfield School and showing him the remarkable works of art being produced there by the pupils. This visit, I learn from *The Northfield Log*, took place in May 1955. Alec admired my father greatly, and they shared many deeply-felt principles regarding education. Both were passionately committed to equal opportunities for all; and nowhere, of course, could this be better exemplified than at Northfield.

Since Edwin Parr has included an excellent appendix in this book, clearly setting out all the major events of my uncle's period as Chief Education Officer for the West Riding, I will not attempt to amplify further. Suffice it to say that I endorse absolutely the general view that Alec was truly a crusading pioneer. He was one of the first to understand that a disadvantaged home environment can fundamentally affect school performance, and was absolutely adamant in his conviction that no child should ever be 'written off as a dud'.

In May 1970, Prime Minister Harold Wilson invited Alec to give the address at Westminster Hall which marked the centenary of the Education Act. He spoke, in large measure, of his concern for those who might not attain their full potential without the assistance and opportunity that a properly designed state education system ought to provide. I was fortunate enough to be present, and it was an occasion that I shall long recall with immense pride.

Much earlier, I had had practical first-hand experience of Alec's compassion. And here I have to admit that, as a schoolboy, I was not blessed with the greatest of mathematical acumen. After one particularly dismal showing, my father set me additional sums in the holidays. My answers, for some reason or other, seemed at variance with those set out in the back of the book. Father was displeased to say the least. 'Ah,' said Alec, coming to the rescue, 'Let me deal with it. Perhaps the book has it wrong.'

What a unique testament James Hutt has given us with *The Northfield Log*. Particularly fascinating is his recreation of school life in the first half of this century. His descriptions of daily routines prior to the First World War are profoundly memorable, especially the period of the 1912 miners' strike, undertaken 'to establish the principle of an average minimum wage for every man and boy working underground'!

It is easy to forget the impact of the coal-mining industry on so very many families in previous generations. Between 1912 and 1920 Mr Hutt brings the industry and those who depended on it vividly to life.

I find *The Northfield Log* continually captivating and, on occasion, deeply moving. It is an important chronicle of local primary education during the last 130 years. No one, surely, who reads this book, can doubt the imperative value of education, so cogently expressed in the quotation Mr Hutt has included from Benjamin Disraeli: 'Upon the education of the people of this country the fate of this country depends.'

Those words, first spoken in the House of Commons over a

FOREWORD

century ago, are no less true today.

I am certain I shall return to *The Northfield Log* many times in the future, and on each occasion silently offer thanks to James A. Hutt.

August 1995

RICHARD ATTENBOROUGH
The Lord Attenborough, C.B.E.

LOCATION OF SOUTH KIRKBY
(not to scale)

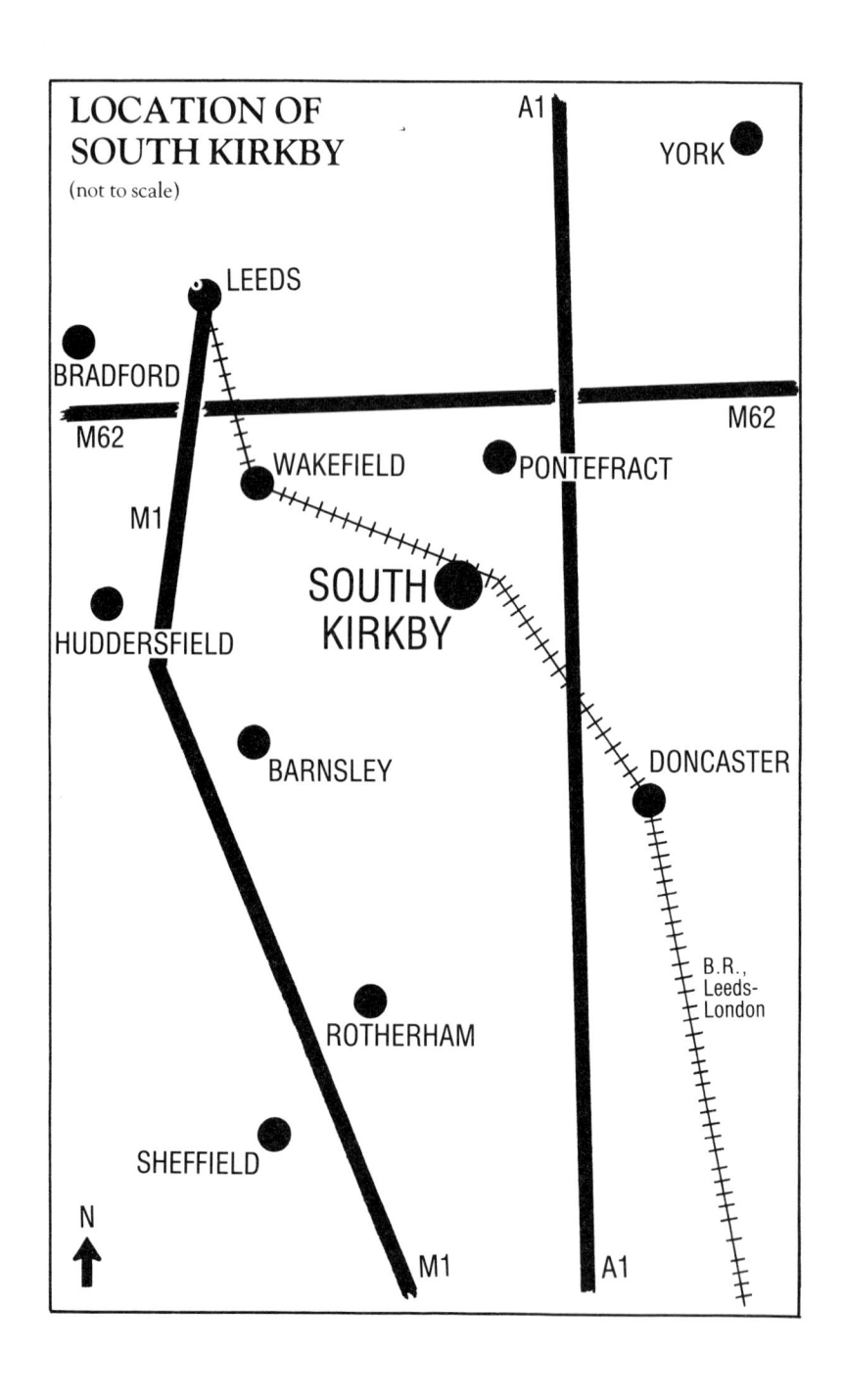

Introduction

To devote a book to the history of a school in a small mining community might seem to many people to be a trifle indulgent. However, several years of research and the author's obvious love of the school have resulted in *The Northfield Log*, which could well be epitomized by Henry James' dictum that 'All human life is there.'

The Northfield Log is an attempt to bring the school — its history and its characters — to life. Basing his work on the actual log books — the school diaries kept by successive headmasters — Jim Hutt has traced the school's development from its birth in a tiny chapel schoolroom in 1902 to the present day. Far from being the sort of dry tome which will merely gather dust on a shelf, this is a vibrant social history, drawing on a variety of authentic anecdotes and events, many of the latter reaching far beyond the classroom.

I must confess to a vested interest. My own involvement with the school is unique, beginning in 1946, when at the age of five I entered Northfield Infant and Junior School. I remained at the school until 1953 when, on passing the 'Eleven Plus', I moved on to Hemsworth Grammar School. After completing my teacher training course I returned to Northfield as a teacher in 1964. There I remained until 1974, when I was appointed to a deputy headship in Doncaster, returning yet again to Northfield in 1978, this time as its head. From pupil to teacher to head — I have grown up with the school.

Northfield has been not only a big part of *my* life; it has played a prominent part in the lives of thousands of South Kirkby people. This book, however, reaches much further. Although it is based on the records of one particular school, it deals with the problems and the pupils, and the highs and the lows of school life, such as might have been encountered in any English school during the last hundred years.

                                  PETER NUTTALL
                                  Head of Northfield Middle School
April 1995   South Kirkby

Acknowledgements

With acknowledgements to the Chief Education Officer of Wakefield M.D.C. for use of information about the Southern Area Review and for permission to make use of the Northfield log books; to Peter Nuttall, Head of Northfield, for his help with Chapter 14; to the staff of Northfield for help with Chapter 13; to Sherilyn Hutt for inclusion of the portrait of J.T. Glover and also for her suggestions regarding material for the cover/jacket.

SOUTH KIRKBY'S SCHOOLS

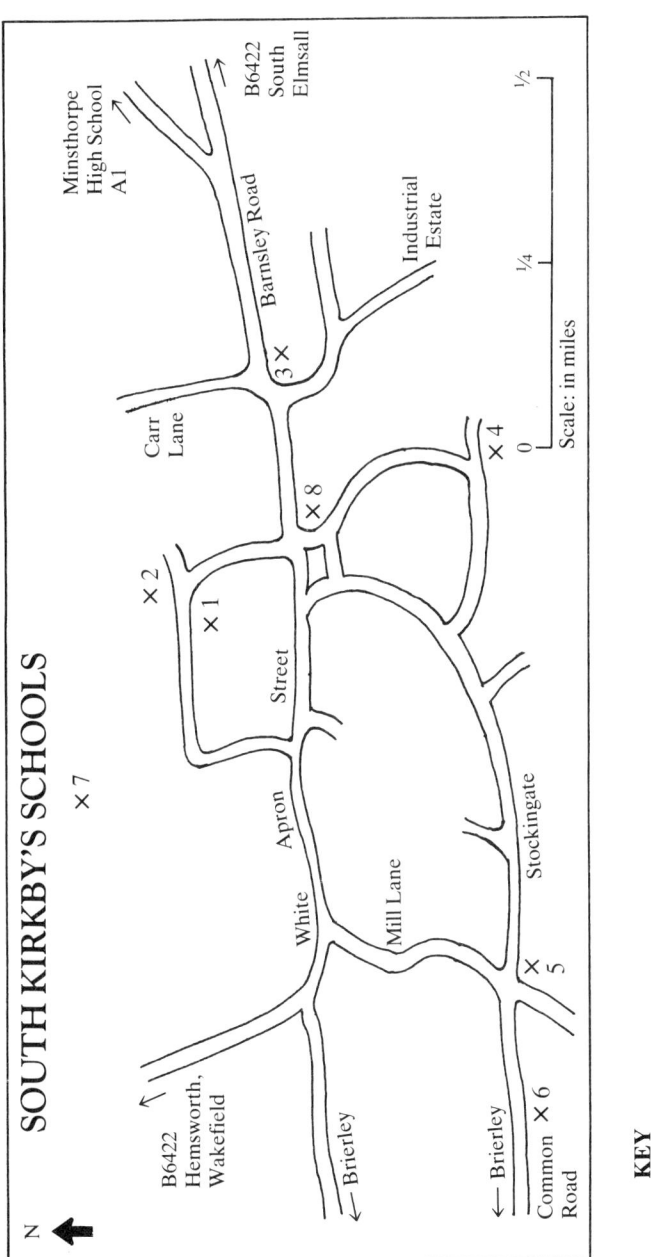

KEY

1. Northfield Middle School
2. Wesleyan Chapel, site of original Northfield School
3. Site of National School
4. Burntwood First School
5. Stockingate First School
6. Common Road Middle and First Schools
7. Site of South Kirkby Colliery
8. All Saints' Parish Church

Northfield Methodist Chapel, where Northfield Board School first opened in 1902

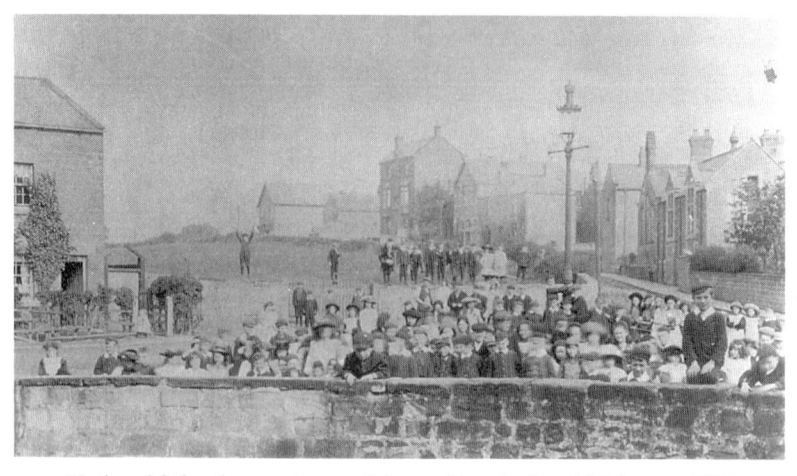

National School, on extreme right, and local schoolchildren, c.1905

1

Pre-History

I ATTENDED the Board School on Northfield Lane, South Kirkby, as an infant towards the end of the Second World War. In 1963 I returned there as a teacher, and remained on its staff until the end of 1992. Even now people stop me in the street and ask, 'Are you still teaching at the Board School?' Or, during the course of reminiscences, some are heard to say, 'I remember when I was at the Board School . . . '

Yet in all its history, spanning ninety years, its official title was 'Board School' for only a very brief period. It opened its doors as a 'Temporary Board School' in 1902, the same year that the Balfour Act abolished School Boards and put elementary education in the care of County Councils.

In the nineteenth century, educational progress in South Kirkby was very slow. It was at the beginning of that century, in 1811, that the National Society was founded. This organization — The National Society for Promoting the Education of the Poor in the Principles of the Established Church (to quote its full title) — promoted the monitorial system popularized by Andrew Bell, an Anglican clergyman, and Joseph Lancaster, a Quaker schoolmaster. Lancaster boasted that, by practising this system, one master could teach up to a thousand pupils. The master would instruct the monitors (selected from the older and more able pupils) in the lesson under consideration; they in turn would duplicate the lesson, each with his or her own allocated group of children, whilst the master maintained overall control. This system was cheap and economical; the annual cost of instructing one child was calculated at a mere 7s. 6d. (37½p).

It was not until 1864, however, that South Kirkby's own

National School was established — by which time Bell and Lancaster and the monitorial system were mere memories. Prior to this date the existence of a state school in the village is doubtful; indeed, the six inches to a mile Ordnance Survey map of 1854 shows no sign of a school, though one of my ancestors, Thomas Hutt, is said to have been in charge of a private school just off White Apron Street, the main thoroughfare, during the second half of the century. There may also have been a 'Dame School' in existence, as *Kelly's Directory* of 1856 lists Mrs Elizabeth Nottingham and Mary Ann Parkin under the heading of 'School'. This sort of establishment was conducted by someone with no teaching experience or qualifications whatsoever, in her own home, for a very small daily or weekly fee.

The National Society being a religious body, the Church had a great influence upon the new National School of 1864. It came to be known locally as the 'Church School'; and Lydgate Hill, where it was situated, became more familiarly known as 'School Hill'. For many years its headmaster was a Mr Schilling; during the period of The Great War he was embarrassed by the Germanic appearance of his name, and consequently dropped the 'c'. His dual role of headmaster and churchwarden was typical of the links forged between church and school in England before the 1870 Education Act.

Scarcely had South Kirkby become accustomed to its new school than the Forster Act of 1870 created a new structure. Not that it made much immediate difference to the community; it was to be another thirty years before its brainchild the Board School was to arrive there.

As a result of the Act, the country was divided into several thousand districts, in each of which the education welfare was to be supervised by a School Board, to be elected by local ratepayers. Each parish was inspected, to assess its existing facilities. Where these were declared insufficient, the voluntary societies and churches were given six months to rectify matters, with a 50% state building grant available only for that duration. Failure to satisfy meant immediate and complete take-over by the new state system. Board Schools received a grant from the government, and a local rate could be implemented to help pay for their upkeep.

The School Board levied a fee of up to 9d. (4p) per week for each child at school. Poor parents were exempt.

As there was the inevitable problem of enforcing the levy and trying to find a satisfactory borderline between payment and exemption, this system was scrapped by the Mundella Act of 1880. State education was now declared completely free. However, the same Act also declared that school attendance was now compulsory for all children between the ages of five and ten. This, too, seemed difficult to enforce. When Northfield 'Board' School opened some twenty years later it was reported that many children of nine, ten and eleven years of age had still never been to school.

In due course educational progress caught up with South Kirkby, coinciding with the dawn of a new way of life, as the agricultural peace of the district came increasingly under threat from industrial interference.

When the National School opened, the population of the village was 482 (1861 census). The school served a predominantly rural community. Before long its peace was shattered by the opening of the railway from Doncaster to Wakefield in 1866. Soon afterwards, plans were afoot to dig for coal in the district. In 1876 two shafts were sunk, and South Kirkby Colliery was born. Privately owned, it nearly died in infancy through bankruptcy, but recovered and produced its first coal in 1883. The small agricultural community was rapidly developing into a substantial mining village.

In the ten years from 1881 to 1891 the population more than doubled from 634 to 1434 and doubled yet again by 1901, when the figure was 2916. The transition which took place comes alive in the following extract from J.S. Fletcher's *A Picturesque History of Yorkshire*, published in 1899:

> South Kirkby, ere the coal days, must have been one of those picturesque villages which one naturally associates with one's notions of sixteenth century life − a cluster of delightfully irregular houses, gardened and orcharded, grouped about a noble church at the foot of which lay a wide stretch of green. The church is still there, handsome and graceful as ever, and all about it are various houses and mansions of stone, but the

outskirts of the village are new and therefore unlovely. Long rows of cottages, each exactly like the other, built of glaring pink brick, without a single redeeming feature or attempt to make them anything but mere shelters, enclose a spot which is naturally one of the most picturesque places in the county. Close at hand is a vast colliery establishment, whose machinery groans and creaks all day and all night, and from which there is continually poured forth clouds of soot and grime and general sombreness. And yet all this modern desecration of Nature's charms cannot wholly destroy the pleasant character of the village, which, in summer, if one can contrive to close one's eyes to the modern abominations, is a very interesting place to visit.

Soon after Fletcher wrote this description, another vast colliery establishment loomed on the horizon in the form of Frickley Colliery. It rapidly became obvious that South Kirkby's tiny Church School was becoming totally inadequate to cater for the huge influx of mining families who were converging on the district.

How the Edwardian teacher dressed.
Mr Schilling and National School staff, 1905

2

South Kirkby Wesleyan Sunday School

DESPITE FOUR EXTENSIONS between 1864 and 1900, the National School continued to burst at the seams as miners poured into the district with their families, seeking employment at South Kirkby or Frickley. As a temporary overflow, two rooms in Northfield Methodist Chapel were converted into a school, bearing the name 'South Kirkby Wesleyan Sunday School'. This 'Temporary Board School', as the log book describes it, opened its doors on 29th September 1902. Although its purpose was to ease the burden imposed on the National School, it seems to have attracted numerous pupils who had never set foot in a school before – or maybe the local attendance officer had been instructed to be especially vigilant on the first day, remorselessly dragging indoors any child found idling in the fields and lanes. The adjacent extract from the first page of the school log book gives a grim impression of the onerous task facing the headmaster.

The 26-year-old headmaster was Frank Williamson, who had been trained at Chelsea in 1895-6. Qualified teachers were very much in a minority. In 1840 Battersea Training College was established by the educationist Kay-Shuttleworth. At that time it was one of only a handful of teacher-training establishments in England. Here, eighteen-year-olds entered for a three year course, probably having already served five years' apprenticeship in schools as pupil-teachers. In 1902, at places like South Kirkby, great reliance was still laid upon pupil-teachers, as three-quarters of all teachers in elementary schools were still untrained. In that year, for instance, training colleges produced 2800 qualified

1902
Sep 29th. This South Kirkby Wesleyan Sunday School was opened this morning as a temporary Board School. Frank Williamson (Chelsea 1895-6) is in charge with Mrs Crossley (Art 50) and Miss Davies (Art 51a) as assistants. 100 children were admitted in the morning and 10 more in the afternoon. The majority of them have been running about the streets for periods varying from 3 mths to 2 years whilst quite a number of children of 9, 10 & 11 years of age, have not yet been to school at all. Insufficient accommodation is the cause of this unsatisfactory state of affairs. The children are wild and coarse in their habits and behaviour and a preliminary test shows the work to be in a very backward state.

First page of the Northfield Log Book, 29th September 1902

teachers but only a quarter of them managed to secure posts. Frank Williamson's two assistants were both untrained — Mrs Clara Maria Crossley from Pontefract, and Miss Mary Davies from Brynmaur, Brecknockshire, South Wales.

Gradually the number on roll swelled from 110 on that first morning to 158 by June 1903, but staff were hard to come by. Williamson had to resort to youth and inexperience — for instance Mary Dickinson of Frickley, who, so the log advises, 'attends on Tuesdays and Fridays but is not counted on the staff.' Maud Reeta Miller was another young teenager, not many years older than the Standard Two children in her charge. She commenced duties in January 1904, and in December of that year she took a scholarship examination at Wakefield. No more than five out of every thousand elementary school pupils managed to gain places in grammar schools at that time. Perhaps she was one of the fortunate few. At any rate, she left Northfield Board School in May 1905. A few months later, Arthur Walker 'commenced duties as monitor.' The log entry for 19th July reads thus: 'Received intimation yesterday that Arthur Walker had been successful at the Intending Pupil Teachership Examination held last May.' He commenced studies at Wakefield Grammar School in September 1906. In October of that same year, Isabella Hirst commenced duties as monitress, her salary being £6 per annum.

When we take into consideration such factors as accommodation and staffing, the conditions in the teaching profession in 1995 must resemble the jolly atmosphere of a holiday camp compared with the grim situation at the turn of the century. The young headmaster, Frank Williamson, had little in the way of trained, experienced staff. Excluding him, the staff-pupil ratio was 1 to 55 in 1902, and only two rooms were available in the temporary accommodation afforded by the chapel. Current class sizes are about 23. They are often rendered even smaller, thanks to the services of part-time assistants. As for experience, the present Northfield staff has accumulated well over two hundred years of teaching service at that school alone.

What might have been the scene on that September morning in 1902 as streams of children thronged and jostled each other into the building? Boys and girls of all ages, from tiny infants to lanky teenagers, swarm into the schoolrooms, creating the utmost noise and confusion. Some are willing pupils, probably having agreed to transfer from the Church School to a place nearer home. Others have perhaps been coerced by their parents, as some children have to be coerced practically every morning. There may be some who have never been to school before, and arrive this morning simply out of curiosity. Some of them certainly had no intention of coming this morning but have been forced into submission by the 'school bobby' – the attendance officer – or by the village policeman, who have been patrolling the lanes and collaring every young person they came across. The majority of the children are poorly clad and ill-shod. Most of the boys are wearing coarse woollen jumpers and tattered trousers or knickerbockers, and the girls are in rough serge dresses and smocks or pinafores. Feet are uncomfortably encased in heavy boots, with many a toe poking through.

The smell of grimy, unwashed, bodies and clothes is becoming stronger by the minute. Gradually, Williamson is able to sort out order from chaos, and makes himself heard above all the din. The name, age and address of each child is registered, and in the process he has the opportunity to observe the unkempt and matted heads of hair, the squinting eyes, the bad and crooked teeth, the runny noses – and a variety of other ailments and deformities.

The school log contains frequent references to matters of health. Between 1902 and 1904, outbreaks of whooping cough, scarlet fever and mumps were recorded. The entry for 25th July 1903 reads:

> I excluded Mary V--- on account of ringworm.

About the same time Williamson wrote:

> I have instructed Lily and Reginald T--- to remain at home for a week as two cases of smallpox have been removed from next door.

The overcrowded conditions in school were hardly conducive to healthy living. The non-flush toilets were situated outside in the yard. The log entry for 3rd October 1902 reads:

> The yard and passages to the offices require some dry ashes.

and on 23rd January 1903 it says:

> The girls' closet has not been attended to as frequently as it ought. I have notified the Scavenger twice and also the Clerk.

The first of His Majesty's Inspectors' reports on the school, the inspection for which was carried out in April 1903, refers to the toilet problem with the remark:

> The seats of the offices are too high for infants, and there is no urinal for infant boys.

School attendance was considerably hampered by illness, and as yet there were no medical inspections in state schools. A degree of success was gained by Williamson in hygiene, however, as the following extracts reveal:

> **25th July 1903**: I warned Mrs W--- about sending Amelia to school in a filthy state.

> **31st July 1903**: I have noticed a decided improvement in above case and also in appearance of other children. Cleaned boots and collars are becoming more in evidence.

The School Board was now taking steps to deal with the other matter affecting attendance — truancy. Under the Balfour Act of 1902, school attendance was made compulsory from five years of age to fourteen. But local authorities could waive this regulation if circumstances warranted it; for instance, if a child had employment to go to. It was up to the locally-elected board to persuade disillusioned or disinclined children (especially those of ten or eleven or more years of age) to attend regularly, or to persuade their parents to get them up in a morning:

> **9th January 1903**: Attendance during the week has not been

satisfactory. Many of the children are being kept at home through the parents not getting up in time to get them off. Ten parents were yesterday summoned before the Board.

3rd April 1903: 24 parents have been written to and 12 summoned before the Board. Mrs B---, whose son John has been playing truant for a month, has to appear before the magistrate at Pontefract.

Much was done to bribe the pupils into maintaining a good attendance record. It might appear to be a contradiction of ideas to persuade children to come to lessons and then reward them with extra playtime, but it seemed to work. On one occasion, 'as a reward, no work was done from 3.15 to 4.00.' On other occasions play was extended from fifteen minutes to half an hour on Friday afternoons for all those pupils with a perfect week's attendance.

Sometimes outside influences became too strong for the children. For example, one entry reads:

A number of children have been absent today on account of pea-pulling.

It is safe to say, however, that today's generation of schoolchildren would no more relish the prospect of a classroom in the middle of August than those pea-pulling pupils of 1903.

Generally the school Board learnt to co-operate with other bodies for the sake of good attendance. The school was always closed on the day of the Miners' Gala and Demonstration. Close ties were maintained with the local chapel, partly as a matter of courtesy, as after all the school was relying on the use of chapel accommodation; a day off was granted for Sunday School Tea Meetings, Sunday School Treats and the like.

There is another noteworthy example of the authorities using their discretion and closing the school completely, rather than risking the humiliation of having empty desks and idle staff. One of the highlights of village life in Edwardian South Kirkby, and elsewhere, was the annual visit of the travelling circus or menagerie. On 6th November 1903 the school was closed half an hour early in anticipation of the effect such an event would have. A few years later, however, on a similar occasion, this spirit of co-operation was apparently forgotten, and twenty children absented themselves for the afternoon.

The pattern of the year's holidays was considerably different from today's. The school year began in April, and in 1903-4 the holidays were as follows:

Whitsuntide:	29th May – 8th June
Midsummer:	27th August – 27th September
Christmas:	23rd December – 11th January
Easter:	25th March – 11th April

Half-term breaks in the autumn and winter terms were not fashionable, and the total of 9½ weeks of holiday time compares with today's total of 13 weeks a year.

At that time pupils were put into standards according to ability; so it was not unusual to find a child confined to the same standard for considerably more than one year, or for one standard to contain children whose age range spanned several years. How humiliating it must have been for a dull twelve-year-old to be held back and educated alongside eight- or nine-year-olds! How awe inspiring it must have been for a bright young thing to be elevated to the ranks of the upper standards, rubbing shoulders with children two or three years his senior!

Re-organization of standards took place after the Easter break, at the beginning of the new academic year. In 1903 the three lowest standards were in the charge of unqualified assistants; the headmaster had charge of Standards 4, 5 and 6, which must have constituted a challenging range of ability and age. The syllabus for that year, annotated in the log book, is divided into six sections. Arithmetic is left curiously vague: 'Scheme B'. English, however, is much more enlightening:

Grammar
Standard 1.	Noun.
Standard 2.	Noun, Verb and Adjective.
Standard 3.	Noun, Verb, Adjective, Adverb, Pronoun. Simple build of sentence.
Standard 4, 5 and 6.	Parsing. Simple sentence analysis. Correction of errors as they occur.

Poetry.

Standard 1.	'Do your best', 'Little things', 'Won't and Will'.
Standard 2.	'The Knowing Chicken', 'Little by little'.
Standard 3.	'Village Blacksmith' (Longfellow). 'Barbara Frietchie' (Whittier).
Standards 4, 5 and 6.	'Revenge' (Tennyson).

Nothing was taught with greater enthusiasm than poetry, though it is doubtful whether the pupils responded with quite the same zeal as they attempted to memorize and then recite in unison the simple Standard 1 choice:

> From a little seed
> A flower grows.
> From a little flower
> A fragrance blows -
> A little fragrance
> That's wafted to me
> As I lie in the shade
> Of the chestnut tree;

or chunks from Tennyson's 'Revenge', which the upper standards had to commit to heart:

> At Flores in the Azores Sir Richard Grenville lay,
> And a pinnace, like a flutter'd bird, came flying from far away.

Whilst such methods of appreciating the arts had the merit of being exercises in discipline, they denied the children the opportunity to express and explore their own imaginations. The same might be said for the art syllabus, which set out to train the eye to see what was there and the hand to draw it precisely and perspectively, but which must have failed to stimulate the pupils' own creativity:

Drawing

Standards 1. and 2.	Simple figures (straight lines). Elements of design.
Standard 3.	Freehand curves. Design.
Standards 4, 5 & 6.	Freehand. Design. Model drawing.

Northfield School still displays three still life objects which were used about that time — a hollow cube, a sphere and a solid flower vase shape.

After two terms, the school received its first visit from His Majesty's Inspectors. What progress might have been expected, I wonder, from a school housed in cramped, temporary, quarters, and run by a young head with an inexperienced female staff, whose pupils were at first sight described as wild, coarse and very backward? The report runs thus:

Year ending April 1903.

This new school is well organised, and, considering the fact that many of the children had little or no grounding when admitted, the work promises well for the future. The staff, however, was a minimum one and not strong on quality during the first part of the year, and the lower grant can only be recommended at the moment. The offices need attention . . .

Presumably His Majesty's Inspector had forgiven Williamson, or had forgotten the incident recorded in the log on 1st December 1902:

B.S. Cornish Esq. H.M.I. called during the dinner hour. He left at 1.50 and was unable to make an entry in the log book owing to the desk keys having been misplaced.

Copy of HMI's Report
   for year ending April 1903.

Mixed School.
   "This new School is well organised, and, considering the fact that many of the children had little or no grounding when admitted, the work promises well for the future. The staff, however, was a minimum one and not strong in quality during the first part of the year, and the lower grant can only be recommended at present. The offices need attention."

Infant School.
   "The school, though newly opened, has had two Head Teachers. Considerable improvement has taken place

under Miss Brown in spite of the children not having previously attended school and of unpunctuality and irregular attendance. The lower grant is recommended at present. The seats of the offices are too high for infants, and there is no urinal for infant boys. As both departments are conducted at present in temporary premises, it is hoped that the building of the new Board School will be proceeded with as soon as possible."

The attendance of the infants appears to have been very irregular. I am to remind the School Board that it is part of their duty" to enforce regularity of attendance.

H.M.I. reports that the offices should be emptied more frequently.

The average attendance of the Mixed School has exceeded the accommodation (Article 85(a) of the Provisional Code).

The Board of Education trust that the new School, for which the plans were finally approved on the 5th June 1903, will be ready for use as soon as possible.

Signed
John Schofield.
Clerk to the Board.

3

A Brand-new School

IT MUST HAVE BEEN with mixed feelings of relief and trepidation that Williamson led his pupils across the road from the chapel to the newly completed school. The new building was based on the traditional Board School plan, popular in the late nineteenth century. There were two departments, a 'Mixed School' and an 'Infant School'. Williamson's Mixed School consisted of a number of classrooms, seven at first, later increased to nine, grouped around a central hall. At opposite ends of the building were two separate entrances, above which were sculpted in sandstone the separate labels 'Boys' and 'Girls'. The boys and girls also had separate ash playgrounds on opposite sides of the building. They were kept apart by a brick wall. In those yards, at the farthest possible point from the main building, were their toilets, usually referred to euphemistically in the log book as the 'offices'.

The log records the transition from chapel to new school in the briefest possible terms:

> **11th April 1904**: Opened school this morning in the new premises.

Nothing more is recorded until the 15th, by which time it is obvious that progress is anything but smooth:

> During this week I have admitted 52 children. The work has been greatly hampered through insufficient stock. New teachers are wanted immediately. Most of my time has been spent in clerical work. Mrs Crossley has had charge of Standards 3, 4, 5 and 6.

In order to ease the strain on Miss Brown (the head of the infant department), 35 of her children were moved up, so that by 4th May a total of 300 pupils appeared on Williamson's register. Yet he still had only three assistants. The overworked head was at considerable pains to combine satisfactorily his clerical duties with his teaching responsibilities. At this time he had three upper standards directly under his charge, and in one instance he 'spent the whole week with Standards 4, 5, 6 and supervising Standard 1.' There were no applicants for posts, and the only respite during the summer of 1904 was on such occasions as this:

> **12th July 1904**: The attendance this afternoon is very poor indeed, only 219 being present out of 315. This is caused by the Church Sunday School Treat which commenced at 2 o'clock.

The immediate crisis was resolved in August by the addition of two extra members of staff, but the major problem of overcrowding was to continue for a long time yet. The steady growth of the local population, and the ever increasing stream of refugees from the Church School (including nine who were expelled from there and placed in an extraordinary 'Standard 0' at Northfield), led to the brand new school rapidly becoming full to overflowing - to such a degree that in 1911 two additional classrooms were built. The following figures give an indication of the escalation in pupil numbers, whilst the number of staff still appeared inadequate to cope satisfactorily:

	Pupils on roll	Permanent staff, excluding head
4th May 1904	300	3
22nd August 1904	316	5
22nd June 1905	391	5
2nd April 1906	376	5
31st March 1909	409	7
4th April 1910	434	7
3rd April 1911	438	8
9th April 1912	497	8

A BRAND-NEW SCHOOL

In 1905 the official maximum accommodation was 360. By 1912 it had been raised to 460, but roll numbers continued to exceed it.

Class sizes were uncomfortably high at the best of times, but often reached ridiculous proportions when there was illness among the staff. The following list shows staffing arrangements and class sizes for 1910-1911.

Class and teacher		Status	Number on register
St. 7	Frank Williamson	H.T.*	14
St. 6	Ignatius Walton	C.A.	40
St. 5	"	"	44
St. 4	Charles Chapman	C.A.	60
St. 3	Mildred Milner	C.A.	59
St. 2a	Clara Cheesborough	U.A.	50
St. 2b	Mrs Clara Crossley	U.A.	47
St. 1a	Mrs Emily Sharpe	C.A.	60
St. 1b	Harriet A. Rothwell	C.A.	60

*H.T. = Head Teacher, C.A. = Certified Assistant, U.A. = Unqualified Assistant.

Small wonder, then, that Williamson was driven despairingly to make such entries in the log as the following:

> **10th April 1905**: I have had charge of St. 1a, 2a, 3 and 4, which is 170 children . . . I cannot bear the continuous strain of maintaining discipline and keeping all at work.

Nearly nine years later the strain was no less acute, according to this entry on 26th January 1914:

> As I am suffering from a bad throat, influenza, cold, headache, toothache etc., I am leaving Mr Chapman in charge and going to bed.

In those Edwardian times the sight of a motor car in South Kirkby was a rarity. Several members of staff reached school by train, and one person journeyed the four miles from Brierley by pony and trap, stabling the pony at the Travellers Inn each day. Several times it was a breakdown in communications which affected staff attendance rather than ill health, as on 8th January 1906:

> Mrs Sharpe did not arrive till 10 o'clock, owing to trap accident. Miss Hinds and Miss Roberts did not arrive till 10.30 owing to missing their train through cab failing in appointments.

As previously observed, Williamson did not spare his own embarrassment in the log book. He dutifully recorded the instances when he himself suffered the indignity of arriving late, as on 11th October 1909:

> I did not arrive till 9.10 this morning owing to a cycle puncture at Hemsworth.

The move to a brand new school did not automatically bring about an improvement in the general health of its pupils. The State seemed to be slow to react to the growing feeling that education for the working classes was linked integrally to their health and their general living condition. Not until 1907 did the Government make medical inspections compulsory in elementary schools. The headmaster at Northfield pre-empted this move by carrying out his own inspection, first recorded on 24th August 1906:

> I spent some time today in examining the children's eyes, throats and teeth. The results will be tabulated in a book for the purpose.

Thereafter, there are several records of visits by local medical practitioners, sometimes to carry out a summary inspection of the pupils and sometimes to inspect specific cases, such as scabies or ringworm. The risk of epidemics, particularly of measles, scarlet fever and whooping cough was high, and between 1904 and 1912 the Medical Officer of Health issued instructions on no fewer than nine occasions to close the school. The longest closure came when the 1911 Christmas holiday lasted until 12th February 1912, 'owing to the prevalence of measles and fever.' Cases of smallpox and diphtheria continued to occur from time to time and there are numerous records of the exclusion of pupils suffering from ringworm and scabies.

In the spring of 1911, however, the school was badly hit by the outbreak of a different complaint – ophthalmia – also known as conjunctivitis. This complaint is highly contagious, and takes the form of inflammation of the eye and the membranes lining the eyelid; and the variety which struck Northfield at this time also gives a pinkish hue to the inflamed eyeball – hence its name, pink-eye.

The first report in the school log was on 7th April:

> The attendance is very much affected just now by Ophthalmia.

Three weeks later it was reported that a number of cases had been excluded. On the 7th May, 17 cases were re-admitted, but there were several fresh exclusions. On the 12th, five weeks after the commencement of the outbreak, there were 78 cases out of 429 on roll. A week later that figure had risen to 101, yet the school remained open. A local doctor visited Northfield and on 24th May the local Medical Officer of Health 'lectured parents on treatment of pinkeye – about 40 present.' Nothing is specified in the log, but maybe the treatment took the form of frequent bathing of the eyes in warm, previously boiled, water – or holding a cotton wool pad soaked in the water against the eye, using some such utensil as a wooden spoon, so as to avoid all contact between eye and finger. The outbreak reached its peak with 116 pupils absent for all of the week ending 26th May. The following week the attendance was a mere 67%. Every room in the school was systematically washed and scrubbed, presumably on the instructions of the M.O.H. Thereafter there was a steady improvement in the attendance, and the disease finally petered out during the course of July.

The inadequacy and unreliability of the heating system scarcely helped to keep the children healthy. Perhaps the headmaster considered that teething troubles were bound to occur in a new school, but his patience must have worn thin as the troubles continued to crop up practically every autumn and winter for the next decade. Williamson's first remark about the heating is on 9th

December 1904:

> The heating apparatus is proving unsatisfactory. The boiler seems altogether inadequate for the work it has to do. I have commenced taking the thermometer readings at 9 a.m. each day.

On 16th January 1905 the highest temperature in school at 9 a.m. was 43°F (51° was the day's highest). By 31st January the problem appeared to have been resolved – 'a leakage in the boiler'. Two years later, however, the heating system was playing up again and obviously puzzling the head with its cantankerous and contradictory behaviour:

> **25th January 1907**: The classrooms have been very cold although the heating apparatus has been drawing well and the pipes have been quite hot.

Thermometer readings at 4 p.m. varied between 49° and 55°F. The following day things were no better and at 9 o'clock Williamson was concerned about how the children were expected to work in temperatures which were not much different from those in the playground.

The catalogue of complaints continues. In October 1907 the log states that 'Messrs Oldroyd's man has added 7lb of mercury to the metal cylinder above the ceiling.' The following winter it is reported that 'water has been dropping from the ceiling under the water cistern. On inspection I find that a joint is leaking and that a considerable quantity of mercury has escaped.' The next day the head dons his caretaker's mantle again:

> Examined apparatus in boiler house and found that seven bucketfuls of water were in the cistern in excess of what was necessary.

In August 1909 it was recorded in the log that the heating apparatus was changed from a high pressure to a low pressure system, a task which had unusual side-effects:

> In consequence of an unauthorised report in the local paper to the effect that in consequence of the alterations not being

A BRAND-NEW SCHOOL 23

completed the schools could not be re-opened, only 57% of the
children are present this morning.

Furthermore – Ada Harper, pupil teacher, was reported unaccountably absent from duties. Four days later she returned, with the following explanation:

> Owing to the newspaper report, she had prolonged her holiday.

Nowadays 62°F is generally regarded as the acceptable working temperature in schools and offices. How cosy and snug such a temperature sounds, compared with the figures quoted in the following report:

> **13th January, 1913**: Today has proved an ideal day for testing the efficiency of the heating apparatus. The ground is deeply covered with snow. The outside temperature remained constant at 32°F till 2 p.m. and then gradually fell to 28° at 4 p.m. There is an entire absence of wind. A heavy fog hangs over the land. The boiler fire has been in all weekend; the caretaker was attending to it at 5.30 this morning. I visited it at 8.45 a.m. and many times since. The draught has been good and a bright glowing fire maintained all day.

Williamson then drew up a chart showing the results of his observations, which is reproduced on the following page.

No doubt a state of cosiness and snugness would have been achieved with less emphasis on ventilation. No doubt also that a certain element, in the form of an icy blast, was required to ensure that the children, starved as many of them were of home comforts, did not nod off in the middle of a lesson.

In October 1913 the head received from the Board of Education a 'Circular on Ventilation', which he dutifully read out to his staff. His statement is recorded in the log book:

> Each class teacher must, either personally or by deputy, see that windows are opened before morning session and that the rooms are flushed with fresh air during recreation and dinner intervals. It is the H.T.'s practice to pay a visit to each room between 9 and 9.30 a.m. to see that the day has started right as regards ventilation.

24 THE NORTHFIELD LOG

So for many years a state of affairs continued to exist whereby a child was either frozen or roasted, depending upon whereabouts he sat in the classroom.

Room	Temperature (°F) 9 a.m. / 11 a.m. / 3 p.m.	State of Radiators	Windows	Ventilators
Central Hall	44 / 47 / 43	hot all day	2 only opened at 11 a.m.	open all day
A	44 / 50 / 52	a) warm b) lukewarm	2 open since 10.30	"
B	46 / 50 / 55	a) hot b) lukewarm c) warm	3 open all day excluding dinner	"
C	50 / 50 / 52	very hot	4 open all day	"
D	46 / 50 / 52	very hot	4 open all day	"
E	50 / 55 / 56	very hot	sliding window open 9.00–9.05 Two all day	"
F	45 / 46 / 48	barely warm	closed and opened many times	"
G	55* / 48 / 47	barely warm	2 open all day	"
H**	46 / 50 / 52	a) very warm b) warm c) warm	4 open since 9. 1 lower window open 1.30–3.30	,
I	45 / 49 / 51	warm	1 open all day, 1 partly open all day	"

* This reading was taken at 9.10 a.m. after 80 children had been in ten minutes and the windows kept closed.
** In this room a pane of glass was out of the door.

Williamson's heating survey. 13th January 1913

4

'How to sustain interest . . .'

QUITE APART FROM the problems of keeping the school fully staffed, ensuring that it was sufficiently warm to work in and that its pupils were in a reasonable state of health, there was the problem of actually teaching the variety of subjects listed in the curriculum. Lack of space, lack of facilities, and lack of expertise among the staff, were bound to hamper progress. Considering the enormous number of pupils in each class, the maintaining of discipline was an almost superhuman task; yet, in essence, the key to the problem was interest. Once the pupils had become interested and attentive, they would have no thoughts about creating havoc in order to relieve their boredom.

In 1906 Williamson began a series of staff discussions, the theme of which was how to make lessons more interesting. He began with discourses on 'How to make Geography lessons more interesting' and 'How to sustain interest in so called dry Geography lessons'. Next came history: 'Conversation among staff on "How to make History lessons more interesting",' which was followed by 'Staff discussion, "Can all History lessons be brightened and illustrated by calling upon children to take some part?" ' Maths was dealt with in just one session: 'Can experimental and practical sums be given to classes of 50 and 60?' Unfortunately the answer is not forthcoming in the log, and it is very doubtful whether one half-hour discussion amongst an inexperienced and overloaded staff would have found a satisfactory solution to that particular problem. Certain it is, though, that proceedings were often hampered by the lack of sufficient stock:

> **27th May 1907**: Stock arrived from Hull today. New stock which should have arrived on April 1st was given out today.
>
> **7th June 1909**: Main stock arrived — we have been without pencils, ink and arithmetic books for many weeks.

What better opportunities could there be for a large class of disinterested rowdies to create havoc?

Good teachers learn to be adaptable and to find ways round awkward situations, as on 28th February 1906, when drill could not take place because the playground was ice-bound. However, 'instead of drill the children have been allowed to slide this morning, the schoolyard being a sheet of smooth ice.' Such unexpected treats enabled the children to see the staff in a different, more humane light, even if it was only for the duration of that session.

A favourite treat at Northfield was lantern slide entertainment. The Magic Lantern is described thus in a contemporary dictionary: 'An instrument for projecting images, figures or pictures in a magnified and intensely bright form on a wall or screen.' At first it was incorporated with Christmas festivities:

> **20th December 1905**: The children have been provided with a Cake Tea and Lantern Entertainment today at a charge of 4d. each. Tea was ready by 4.30. From 5 to 5.30 the children amused themselves with games. From 5.30 to 6.15 they were entertained by their teachers. From 6.15 to 8.15 over 250 views were thrown on the screen.

It became an annual event. A programme of the slides used at the Christmas Entertainment of 1907 reads as follows:

> 230 slides used — Wonders of the World 60 — Merchant of Venice 26 — Cinderella 12 — Beauty and the Beast 12 — Jack and the Beanstalk 12 — Jack the Giant Killer 10 — History of the Butterfly 10 — Excelsior 10 — Aesop's Fables 30 — Humorous 48.

The educational value of the Magic Lantern was quickly realized. The cinema was becoming popular in the towns, but South Kirkby never acquired its own cinema until the 1920s. The Magic Lantern was the next best thing to silent movies, and children were so fascinated by this contraption that they would quite happily watch anything for hours on end. Williamson was quick to take advantage of their natural reaction, using slides to illustrate history, geography and nature lessons and also as a reward for 100% attendance. But even the Magic Lantern's magic failed occasionally:

> **2nd March, 1910**: Lantern Entertainment for upper standards could not be given owing to empty cylinder of oxygen being sent instead of full one.

On 13th February 1913 oxygen was made redundant:

> The timetable was modified today to enable each class to view 50 slides and have a lesson on Britannia's Realm. The lantern was illuminated with acetylene gas for the first time with good results.

Any amount of modification of the timetable was to be encouraged if it broadened the scope of a somewhat restrictive curriculum. Such an example occurred in 1910 when Arthur Rhodes, a former South Kirkby pupil, was persuaded to give a lecture on life in South Africa, where he was employed in the Rand Gold Mine. From August 1913 the normal timetable was scrapped one afternoon each week for groups of boys and girls of the upper standards, to enable them to walk the 1½ miles to the new school in Westfield Lane, South Elmsall, to participate in Handicraft and Housewifery classes.

The Temperance Movement, born in middle-class Victorian society, found an annual place on the schedule. The first temperance lesson is recorded in the log in 1914, and Williamson encouraged its survival at Northfield for many years.

The greatest treat for the children, and the most positive break from the constraints of the timetable, was a school outing. At first a group of pupils might be taken into the neighbouring field or lane to explore the hedgerows and pursue a discourse on nature in the environment. From these humble beginnings more ambitious projects gradually developed. The first record of a school outing venturing beyond the village of South Kirkby is on 16th July 1905, when 75 of the senior children were escorted to the village of Kirk Smeaton, some eight miles distant. The event is described only as 'an unqualified success'. It was a pleasantly situated place in open countryside, untainted by brooding colliery buildings and unscarred by endless rows of colliers' terraced homes, but the most likely destination for the school party would be the nearby Brockadale Woods, clothing the narrow valley of the River Went. Its romantic associations, being in fox-hunting country and in an offshoot of Sherwood Forest, no doubt added to its charm for a party of pit-village urchins. Furthermore, it was, as its name suggests, a haven for badgers, and even otters used to be abundant on the banks of the stream.

Two years later a train excursion was arranged to Adwick-le-Street, situated on the old Roman road from Doncaster to Castleford. Its links with the Romans, and possibly also its American associations as the burial place of a member of the Washington family, may have made it a profitable educational venue. Prior to the advent of the nearby colliery and all its ugly appurtenances, it was in an attractive rural setting. Maybe the biggest attraction of such an outing, however, was the opportunity to travel on a railway train — for many children a unique experience at that time.

Similar educational and recreational ventures followed, to such destinations as Pontefract Castle and Pontefract Park. Then, in 1911, came the first excursion to the seaside. It was so successful that it became an annual event. Bridlington was the first venue — and Scarborough, Cleethorpes and Skegness were later choices. No details are expressed in the log, other than comments about the weather, until 25th June 1920, when the following description was entered:

> School excursion to Scarborough. This school joined with Moorthorpe Boys — 368 children. Left Moorthorpe Station 8 a.m. York 10 a.m. Arrived Scarborough 11.20. Left Scarborough 8.05. York 9.30. Pontefract 10.45 p.m. A special engine brought the coaches from Pontefract, for which a special fee of £6 had to be paid.

Some of the sweetest treats were those which were, to the

children, quite unexpected. For instance:

16th June 1911: Schools closed for Coronation Holiday.

27th June 1911: A packet of sweets was given to each child yesterday under instructions from the Coronation Committee.

13th July 1911: Coronation mugs and confectionery bags distributed this afternoon.

Other occasional holidays which came out of the blue were for the Rural Education Exhibition at Barnsley and the Doncaster Royal Agricultural Show in 1912, and for South Kirkby's own Agricultural Show in 1914.

Each year there was held somewhere in the district a Miners' Demonstration. One can imagine how difficult it was for the pupils to restrain wild whoops of delight as they heard the Head declare solemnly, 'School will be closed on Monday June 21st on account of the Miners' Demonstration in Sheffield.' Very few children would attend the event twenty miles away, but none would regret or waste the opportunity to cavort in the fields and lanes in the summer sunshine, leaving thoughts of an overcrowded and claustrophobic classroom behind for just one Monday. A similar reaction would be generated by the announcement that 'The school will be closed tomorrow, the polling day for the Parliamentary Election of the Osgoldcross Division.' The fact that the children probably had no idea why they were being granted an extra day's holiday was by the way.

The new school was now playing an increasingly active part in the community. It had come to be regarded unofficially as a community centre for the village of South Kirkby, and its premises were made available for a wide variety of activities outside of school hours.

In 1906 Evening School courses commenced, offering (among other subjects) adult tuition in reading. The following year a Mining class commenced, and in 1913 Surveying was added to the curriculum. The local choral society held its concerts at Northfield, and another annual event held there was the 'Tradesmen's Concert'. Church functions, such as the annual Christmas Bazaar, were allowed use of the premises. Under Williamson's leadership and encouragement the Board School staff occasionally relaxed from the daily strain of the classroom by holding such events as a Christmas Staff Social and Dance – and in 1913, so the log book records, they took part in a tennis match with the Broad Lane staff from South Elmsall, followed by a similar event with the Hemsworth Southmoor Road staff.

Open Days became a regular feature, when parents were encouraged to visit the school to review a display of the pupils' work. The children were allowed to show off to their parents in a different manner at the annual school concert. This extract from the log describes one such event:

> **18th November 1909**: The children gave a concert last night. It consisted of an operetta entitled 'Snow White and the Seven Dwarfs' and a sketch entitled 'Judge Pro-Tem'. The premises had to be specially licensed for this play.
>
> **19th November 1909**: The Concert will be repeated tonight for the children of the village. The charge will be 1*d*. for children and 3*d*. for adults.

The school could not help but be influenced and affected by outside activities. If there was a church bazaar it affected Northfield because it required the use of the school premises. If the travelling circus was in the district the school attendance was affected. For the Coronation of George V in 1911 a holiday was declared. Election Day was also a national holiday. And if there was a miners' strike the repercussions in school were unavoidable.

South Kirkby c.1914, Rose & Crown Inn on right.
The main access to Northfield was by the central path to the left.

South Kirkby c.1914, parish church in centre, taken from village green.

5

The Miners' Strike of 1912

THE FIRST MENTION in the log book about the 1912 Miners' Strike is on 19th March, though the strike actually commenced on 1st March. There had been plenty of warning given to the public as a whole and to the Government in particular, for the Miners' Federation of Great Britain, having held a ballot which declared overwhelming support for a strike, had given notice on 18th January of impending action. The fundamental principle for which the M.F.G.B. was fighting on behalf of the country's miners was the Minimum Wage Principle, 'to establish the principle of an average minimum wage for every man and boy working underground.' A minimum day-wage rate of 7s. 6d. (37½p) was stipulated in the Yorkshire area for the piece-working coal-getter at the coal-face. A minimum of 5s. (25p) was stipulated for all adults, and 2s. (10p) for boys. The vulnerability of the collier's financial status was illustrated by a South Wales delegate to the M.F.G.B. at a special conference held on 14th November 1911:

> Take the case of a colliery labourer with a standard of 3s. per day, plus fifty per cent, or 4s.6d. per shift. This makes for a full week's work 27s., but he does not work full; there is the slack time, trade and general holidays to be taken into account, which will reduce the average from six days to five and a half per week and reduces his average wages from 27s. to 24s.9d. per week. Let us look now at the family budget, which will work out at something like this for a family of six persons. Rent 6s. per week, coal 1s.6d., fuel 1s., clothing and footwear 5s., club doctor and Federation 1s. per week, making a total of 14s.6d. This leaves 10s.3d. per week for food to feed six persons for a

week. Allowing a bare three meals per day, eighteen meals per week — 126 meals for the family — with 123 pence to pay for them, or less than 1d. per meal per head.

Have we overstated the case? No; if anything it is understated. There are thousands in this movement that are existing for less than 1d. per meal per head.

At that time all mines were still in private ownership. The coal-owners refused to negotiate, sticking by their own principle, which amounted to 'a fair day's wage for a fair day's work.' Herbert Asquith's government intervened in a vain attempt to avert the halt in production of coal, which would rapidly drain the life-blood of Britain's industry.

On 1st March a million miners came out on strike. The people of South Kirkby, practically all of them dependent on the local mines for their livelihood, found their financial resources steadily dwindling away, for the strike pay of around ten shillings a week was a poor substitute for a normal wage. There was a good deal of poverty around at the best of times and now, as Williamson couldn't help noticing through the pupils of his school, conditions were becoming desperate:

> **19th March 1912**: 50 children sent to school this morning breakfastless, owing to Miners' Strike, which commenced March 1st. 20 children who stated they had no bread in the house were fed at my expense. The other 30 who stated they had bread at home were sent home for it with instructions to return at once.

Despite the shortage of money to buy bread, '235 children during the weekend have had money given to them to spend on sweets,' observed the head the following day.

For the next few weeks Williamson kept a daily account of the number of children fed in school, initially at his own expense, occasionally through the charity of others — '5 were fed on scones kindly sent by Mrs Forrest' — and later under the 1906 Provision of Meals Act.

The Act permitted Local Education Authorities to make available existing premises, equipment and staff for the provision of meals in schools. It was necessary to institute a charge unless parents were actually unable to pay. This provision, however, was only spasmodically taken up, and in 1912 there was no provision of meals on a general scale.

The Miners' Strike of 1912 was the first time that the Act was invoked in South Kirkby. The assistance was only for the benefit of necessitous children, and took the form of the supplying of breakfasts rather than midday meals. An entry made by Williamson in similar circumstances during the Miners' Strike of 1926 describes these breakfasts:

> Each child was supplied with a milk scone, an iced bun and a mug of cocoa.

The feeding of children reached its peak at the beginning of April. For the next three weeks the daily number varied between 142 and 153. The Easter vacation was curtailed to enable children to be breakfasted in school. Only Good Friday and Easter Monday were given. Eventually it was recorded:

> **19th April 1912**: Tomorrow (Saturday) is the first pay day after the Strike. Consequently breakfasting at school is to be discontinued.

On 29th March Prime Minister Asquith had announced that the Government would be introducing a bill compelling mine owners to pay a minimum wage. The Coal Mines (Minimum Wage) Act of 1912 was to 'provide a Minimum Wage in the case of Workmen employed underground in Coal Mines . . . and for purposes incidental thereto.' Once adopted, the Bill stood on the Statute Book until 1947. Resumption of work had been advised on 4th April. The Yorkshire and Lancashire areas were dubious and reluctant to go back, but by mid-April most of the pits in the country had resumed, including Frickley and South Kirkby.

As it turned out, the local miners were right to be dubious. According to the terms of the Act, each District Board could set its own minimum rate higher or lower than the recommended general district rate. Most District Boards settled for a minimum less than the 5*s*. stipulated by the Federation. The disgruntled miners were now back at work, feeling that the biggest strike ever staged in Britain had achieved for its protagonists less than nothing.

South Kirkby Colliery

*Eight hours' work,
Eight hours' play,
Eight hours' sleep,
And Eight bob a day.*

Essay title and rhyme which formed part of exhortation to miners to strike in 1912.

6

The Great War

THE DAY FOLLOWING the event which precipitated half the world into the Great War – the assassination of Archduke Francis Ferdinand, heir to the Austrian Empire – South Kirkby Council School's log stated simply:

> **29th June 1914**: Mr Todd resumed duty ... [after illness]

When the news came through that on 23rd July Austria had issued a final ultimatum to Serbia, the log stated:

> The school will be closed on Monday next for the South Kirkby Agricultural Show.

On 28th July Austria declared war on Serbia, on 30th July Russia mobilized her army in Serbia's defence, and on 1st August (following Germany's invasion of Belgium) Great Britain declared war on Germany. None of these events is recorded in the school log. The foreboding and gloom had been intensifying for a long time, despite local people's efforts to pretend that the outside world's horrors didn't exist. As far as events at Northfield were concerned, the everyday matters pertaining to school life were all-important, and the place remained completely unaffected by the world crisis developing beyond its walls.

There came a time, however, when world affairs could not be excluded any longer, and the first hints of the war began to creep into the entries in the log. In August, Germany's invasion and occupation of Belgium had been completed swiftly and without mercy, despite the presence of 70,000 British troops. On 8th October the realities of this horrific conflict were finally dawning

THE GREAT WAR 39

on people in Britain, and it was recorded in the log:

> Collection today among staff realized £1 for Belgian Relief
> Fund.

Life in Britain must have been strange during those early days of the war. All hell was being let loose just across the English Channel, yet people here were still doing their best to lead normal lives. The usual Summer holidays had been taken, and shops were assuring customers of business as usual. There was a great deal of gossip and discussion about events described in the newspapers, but the inevitable feelings of excitement must have been predominantly as detached spectators rather than participants. One way or another, however, local people gradually became involved:

> **9th November 1914**: The children were assembled on the Green
> at 9.40 this morning to give a send-off to the recruits for the
> Miners' Battalion. They were back at work again at ten o'clock.

There was a steady stream of enlisters from the mining fraternity during the first year of the war. Before August 1914 the total number of miners in Great Britain stood at 1,116,648. By August 1915 over a quarter of a million had enlisted.

Before long, the school's staff were affected by the war:

> **7th June 1915**: I was absent from school from 10 a.m. on a visit
> to Wakefield re. a call to military service.

> **8th June 1915**: I was absent from 2.20 owing to appointments
> with dentist and Major Smith at Pontefract Barracks.

> **10th June 1915**: I shall be absent again from 9.40 owing to a
> second appointment with the dentist and Major Smith at
> Pontefract.

However, Frank Williamson remained at his post in South Kirkby for the duration of the war. Three other members of the staff enlisted. Arthur Street, aged 21, left on 11th February 1916 'to join the Colours.' A few weeks later he was followed by

Joseph Edward Mark Todd, a 27 year old from Northallerton, who 'joined the R.F.A.' (Royal Fleet Auxiliary) and was dispatched to France. Finally Charles Chapman joined up on 9th June 1916. Originally from Croydon, he came to South Kirkby to teach at Northfield in 1909. Now he left to fight with the Northumberland Fusiliers in France. Todd and Chapman both resumed their teaching careers at South Kirkby on 3rd February 1919, but Arthur Street never returned from the war.

Meanwhile Williamson had problems – how to keep South Kirkby Council School going on a skeleton staff. In April 1915 there were 500 pupils on roll. The staff consisted of head, five qualified and two unqualified teachers. When Todd, Chapman and Street left, a total teaching staff of five remained. Every effort was made to recruit extra staff, little matter how temporary or inexperienced, but the strain of trying to cope obviously took a severe toll on the health of the teachers at Northfield, judging by the almost daily absence report in the log during the summer of 1916:

> **10th July 1916**: Miss Lawson begged for leave to accompany lady friend to Liverpool to visit her husband dangerously wounded in hospital.
>
> **11th July 1916**: Miss Lawson not returned. Miss Widdowson absent ill. Mrs Sharpe did not commence till 10 a.m. owing to sickness.
>
> **12th July 1916**: Miss Widdowson resumed. Miss Lawson not yet resumed.
>
> **13th July 1916**: Miss G. Harrison absent. Miss Lawson still absent.

While one sort of struggle was raging across the Channel, the children of Northfield were engaged in a different struggle – trying to cope with the name of one of the temporary recruits to the staff. She was Miss Phyllis Thistlethwaite.

An attendance of only 66% one particular day in November 1916 might have been expected to bring temporary relief to a stressed staff, but the circumstances were full of foreboding.

THE GREAT WAR

Williamson began his entry in the log: 'Owing to Zeppelin Raid overnight . . . ' These dirigible airships made several raids over eastern England in 1916, and their menace had been experienced at Scarborough on the Yorkshire coast. But this was the first recorded incident over South Kirkby. The main target was the local collieries, but these raiders were both indiscriminate and inaccurate, so the general public was considerably at risk. However, the 66% attendance at school the day after the raid was no reflection on casualties, but merely a reflection on the number of excited children who had been up half the night watching these silent and sinister raiders, and who were consequently catching up on their lost sleep at the school's expense.

Gradually Britain's air-force and her anti-aircraft guns learnt to cope effectively with the Zeppelin menace. A series of Zeppelin disasters occurred during 1917 and a large war-plane known as the Gotha took its place. South Kirkby's next taste of war action came in September of that year:

> **25th September 1917**: There is a very poor attendance this morning. The whole village has been in a disturbed and excited state during the night on account of an air-raid and doubtless many children have been out during the night.

From the moment that the Board School had given its official send-off to the Miners' Battalion, the spirit of patriotism was fostered and encouraged. A branch of the War Savings Association was opened in school in October 1916, and its success can be gauged by the following entries:

> **12th March 1917**: Twenty five new members for War Savings Association.

> **8th March 1918**: A great effort has been made this week in connection with the War Savings Association; the subscriptions have been trebled.

Another example of instilling a loyal interest in Britain's progress on the war front is this entry dated 21st December 1917:

> School assembled at 9 a.m. An address given on exploits of

W.R. (West Riding) regiments before Cambrai. Dismissed at 9.30 for extra day's holiday.

(The Battle of Cambrai, in northern France, began victoriously for Britain on 20th November 1917, when the Royal Tank Corps made a successful assault on German lines. There was insufficient back-up, however. Trench warfare ensued for the next ten days, each side losing about 45,000 men, and neither side gaining a clear advantage.)

The school's art work was another example of patriotic fervour. On 17th June 1917 some drawing specimens were submitted to an art exhibition held at Westfield Lane School, South Elmsall. Amongst a proliferation of still-life subjects typical of the period were the Union Jack and a shiny pair of army boots. The mounted display has stood the test of time and can still be seen at Northfield School.

The week beginning 18th March 1918 was described in the logbook as 'Aeroplane Week, when the village attempts to raise £12,500 for War Loans. At 4 p.m. this school combined with the Church School in parading the village . . . This school is aiming at reaching £500.' That figure proved too ambitious for such a poor working class village as South Kirkby then was, but the £379 raised was nevertheless a worthwhile effort.

Shortly after that entry the log book was filled. It had lasted from the inception of the school in 1902. A new permanent log was not immediately available, as the following entry explains:

> Owing to paper shortage due to war, this school has been
> without Log Book from September 2nd to present time. Notes
> during this interval have been made in an exercise book.

A new log was opened on 2nd June 1919.

When the Armistice was declared on 11th November 1918, signifying the end of four years of bitter and bloody war, there was great rejoicing throughout the world. Eight million people had been killed in the fighting, and many millions more suffered as a consequence of the war. Now it was all over and there was every reason for celebration. However, no celebrations took place at South Kirkby Council School. It was closed because of a devastating influenza epidemic. The school was first ordered to be closed on 9th July 1918. It re-opened on 2nd September, only to be closed again on 28th October for a further five weeks. There followed a brief respite, but then matters took a turn for the worse, as may be gathered from the entries in the log for the week beginning 10th March 1919:

> **10th March**: Mr Todd, Mr Chapman, Miss Widdowson, Miss Wilcock absent – influenza.
>
> **11th March**: Mr Chapman, Miss Widdowson, Miss Wilcock, Miss Eckersley absent – influenza.
>
> **12th March**: Mr Chapman, Miss Widdowson, Miss Wilcock, Miss Eckersley, Miss Harrison absent – influenza.
>
> **13th March**: Ditto.
>
> **14th March**: Ditto.

Inevitably, with the staff attendance at 55% and the pupils' attendance recorded at 77.5% for that week, the school was doomed for closure yet again, this time for a fortnight.

The great influenza epidemic of 1918-19 was the scourge of Europe. Nicknamed 'Spanish 'Flu' and 'The Spanish Lady', it took advantage of many war-weary and debilitated nations. In Britain alone, over 229,000 people died of it, many of them from South Kirkby, some even from its school. Amongst the victims was Miss Widdowson, whose death occurred on 15th March. Celebrations to mark the end of the war, therefore, were belated:

> **21st July 1919**: On Saturday July 19th these premises were used in connection with the national peace festivities. The children from three upwards received a tea on these premises. Sports were held in Mr Askham's field. Medals are to be distributed later.
>
> **25th July 1919**: The schools close today for the Summer Vacation, which has been extended to five weeks by the addition of one week for the celebration of peace.

The school was in session on 11th November 1919, and the occasion was marked thus:

> This day – Armistice Day – was duly observed, in accordance with the King's wishes, by a suspension of all work for a space of two minutes as a tribute to the memory of the Dead.

Frank Williamson, ever precise in word and deed, added:

> The timetable was altered slightly. The children assembled at 10.55. Recreation was from 11.05 to 11.30.

7

The 1920s
Period of Poverty

EXTERNAL EVENTS continued to have a marked effect on life in school. The first reference to the prolonged miners' strike of 1921 ran thus:

> **14th April 1921**: This is the second week of the miners' strike. One boy fainted during prayers this morning, which suggests that some children may not be getting sufficient nourishment, though none, as yet, have come breakfastless.

The Great War was followed by a brief boom in trade. By the end of 1920 that boom was in decline, world trade slumped, and Britain's unemployment figures practically doubled in the space of four months, standing at over 1¼ million by March 1921. The Government, which had supervised coal production and wages since 1917, decided to de-control the coal industry, which in effect would mean a considerable cut in miners' wages. They would now be deprived of the three shilling War Wage, as well as the Sankey Commission Award of two shillings a shift. As had been expected, at the beginning of March, the coal owners — the Mining Association of Great Britain — announced a termination of all contracts from the end of the month. The new terms offered varied from one area to another according to the generosity of each District Association, but in all cases wage reductions were huge, some districts cutting wages by almost a half. The Miners' Federation of Great Britain appealed in vain to the Government for a subsidy to maintain their standards and for the creation of a National Wages

Board. Then the M.F.G.B. instructed all miners to allow their notices to lapse. This included such workers as engine-men and pump-men. Without their work the condition of the pits would rapidly deteriorate. The mine-owners declared a lock-out. Thus, on 31st March 1921, the Government ceased to control the mines; a million miners were idle, locked out, and their dependants began to suffer.

Slowly but surely hardship gripped the miners and their families. Three weeks into the strike, Williamson recorded in the log:

> The Coal Strike continues. No actual poverty yet noticed among the children.

And a week later:

> The Coal Strike continues. No general poverty yet. One boy only has been discovered breakfastless.

No doubt everyone in the mining community was expecting the miners to achieve a swift victory. The strike was five weeks old when it was recorded:

> **5th May 1921**: Children have been fed today at a Soup Kitchen opened near the Vicarage and supported voluntarily.
>
> **13th May 1921**: The children are being provided with a mid-day meal of soup and bread at the Vicarage buildings.

Two weeks later:

> **27th May 1921**: The Coal Strike continues and the feeding of children continues and increases.

The emergency of 1921 saw the most extensive provision of meals since the Act of 1906 had come into force. Notwithstanding the gifts of food by relief organizations, the cost of meals provided was put at £10,642 by the West Riding Education Committee, who were entitled to recover the costs from parents – unless it was obvious that they were in no position to pay. Only just over £6,500 was recouped by the Committee.

THE 1920s — PERIOD OF POVERTY

In an effort to break the protracted deadlock and persuade the miners to resume work, Lloyd George's Government dangled the carrot of a subsidy before their noses — but not a subsidy which would restore their wages to the pre-March level. The offer was of ten million pounds to prevent large reductions, with the guarantee that initially there would be no greater reduction than three shillings a shift. Considering that a miner's daily wage at the beginning of 1921 was not much over ten shillings, this would indeed be a great reduction. The miners resisted temptation for week after week, despite numerous threats from Lloyd George to withdraw the offer of ten million pounds. Eventually the prolonged poverty forced the miners to submit. In July they resumed work, having gained nothing except the knowledge that they had the determination and the will — as well as the cause — to fight again.

> **1st July 1921**: The Coal Strike, having lasted thirteen weeks, ceases tomorrow. The pits reopen on Monday.

Four years later the miners and the Government — this time Baldwin's Conservative Government — were heading towards confrontation again. As a result of the restoration of the value of the pound to its 1914 level by the Chancellor of the Exchequer, Winston Churchill, money flowed freely into London's money market; but prices of exports rose, coal became very difficult to sell, and once again the mine owners decided that wage cuts were called for. The miners were aggrieved, and called on the support of their closest trades union allies, the railwaymen and the transport workers. A general strike loomed. Baldwin tried to head it off by giving the mine-owners a subsidy for one year, on condition that there would be no strikes or wage cuts, and the Samuel Commission was appointed to investigate the problems besetting the industry.

The Commission reported in favour of major reforms in the administration of mines, but also in favour of wage cuts. The miners rejected its findings. Negotiations between the Trades Union Congress and the Government failed. The country was plunged into the General Strike on 4th May 1926.

Copy. H.M.J.'s Report.   19/10/22.

Acc.ⁿ   S.G 150   Av. att 108
         M. 460   312
         I. 360   262

Report by Mr J.H. Brown, H.M.J.
    Inspected on 19th September, 1922.
Mixed.

The very difficult staffing conditions during recent years have made exacting demands on the head teacher who deserves praise for the admirable spirit with which he has endeavoured to meet the situation. A settled and suitable staff has now been secured so that it should be possible to raise the present unsatisfactory standard of attainment to a satisfactory level. But, to secure this, the staff, who show much enthusiasm and industry, will need to revise curriculum and methods of presentation. At present there is too much that is dull and uninspiring, hence the response of the children mentally and in their written work is not commensurate with their abilities.

In English too much effort is concentrated on the formal side. It would be well for the teachers to study carefully the Board's latest suggestions on the teaching of English.

Arithmetic is not adequately based on the experience and interests of the children, and the pupils are consequently dull and unresponsive when given simple exercises based upon their daily experiences.

History and Geography also show evidences of failure on the part of teachers to discriminate between lessons that the children can appreciate and assimilate and those that leave them mentally apathetic.

In all lessons it is desirable that expression work, in the form of notes, composition, maps, sketches, etc should be adequately provided for, as a test of the child's appreciation and industry, and as an indication of the form succeeding lessons should take.

Charles J. Crosby DI.
3/11/22

As far as Frank Williamson was concerned, the crisis centred entirely on whether or not the members of staff turned up for work as usual, if the log book is anything to go by:

> **4th May 1926**: A General Strike commences today. Trains and all means of transport are at a standstill. Mr Chapman arrived at 9.30.
>
> **5th May 1926**: Mr Chapman arrived at 10.15.

The T.U.C. suddenly called off the General Strike on 12th May, with no conditions. The miners expressed surprise and dismay as they prepared to fight on alone, the declaration from the Secretary of the Miners' Federation, Arthur Cook, ringing in their ears and spurring them on to victory:

> Not a penny off the pay, not a minute on the day.

The miners stayed out for seven months. At first they could endure the struggle without too much hardship:

> **31st May 1926**: No signs yet of underfeeding or physical deterioration. No boy has come without breakfast this morning.

But soon the tally of breakfastless children began, and it increased steadily:

> **7th June 1926**: Five children came to school last week either without breakfast or having had insufficient through shortage. They were provided for at school.
>
> **11th June, 1926**: Ten children breakfasted today. Each child was supplied with a milk scone, an iced bun and a mug of cocoa.
>
> **17th June 1926**: 21 children breakfasted today.
>
> **23rd June 1926**: 42 children breakfasted today.

Apart from the emergency arrangements organized by the education authority, and the gifts of food provided by local charity, international support spurred the miners on to tolerate these

THE 1920s — PERIOD OF POVERTY

difficult times. By the end of August, £879,000 had poured into the Miners' Relief Fund, over half of which came from the trades unionists of the U.S.S.R. In the circumstances, however, with over one million miners and their dependants to consider, such a vast sum as that didn't go far. Luxuries were out of the question, of course, and even some basic necessities had to be overlooked. As summer passed into autumn, warm clothes, boots and heating became increasingly hard to come by:

> **28th October 1926**: Today we are without coal and coke. The heating apparatus is not in use. Fortunately the weather is comparatively mild. The rooms of the main building stood at 45°, 48°, 48° and 48°F at 9 a.m. The rooms of the hut were much lower, registering 40°, 44° and 41°. As there was a prospect of the sun breaking out and the temperature rising, I determined to carry on . . . At 10.30 a load of coke arrived and fires were at once lit in the hut rooms.
>
> **29th October 1926**: The attendance is very low indeed [probably through so many children shivering at their desks the previous day], mainly due to shortage of boots and clothes owing to the continuance of the strike, which is now in its 26th week.
>
> **3rd November 1926**: Today being mild, the fires were allowed to go out at 9.30 a.m. One load of outcrop coal was delivered on Monday. It is almost finished, having very poor heating properties.
>
> **12th November 1926**: This week has been comparatively mild and quiet. There has been no heating trouble. Several loads of 'outcrop' coal have been secured. Two loads of firewood and some coke have been delivered. 87 children have been breakfasted this week.

During the autumn there was a trickle of miners returning to work, mostly in the Midlands. By the beginning of September 400 Yorkshire miners had returned, and by 3rd October 3,598 had returned out of a total workforce of 150,000. The vast majority remained on strike until the bitter end.

Between them, the Government and the mine-owners achieved another overwhelming victory over the miners, the most resolute of whom finally capitulated on 30th November. Their seven months of suffering was yet again in vain. Through hardship they were forced back to work to face more years of lower wages, longer hours, increasing threat of unemployment in the industry, and a steadily deteriorating standard of living. In mining villages like South Kirkby, malnutrition and general deprivation set in on an even wider scale as average wages per man-shift slumped from 10s.5d. (52p) at the beginning of 1926 to 10s. in 1927, and then to 9s.2½d. in 1929. According to the school log, conditions reached their nadir in the winter of 1928-29. A depressing series of entries runs thus:

> **14th December 1928**: Dr Stoddart examined malnutrition cases.
>
> **18th December 1928**: List of children recommended for feeding sent off this morning.
>
> **20th December 1928**: Feeding utensils, dried milk and biscuits arrived at 5.15 p.m. today.
>
> **7th January 1929**: 33 pairs of boots (under Sir James Hinchcliffe Fund) have been received from County Hall. They are only half the number asked for, and cannot be distributed, as lists have not been returned. [Sir James Hinchcliffe was chairman of the West Riding County Council during the 1920s.]
>
> **10th January 1929**: As there is much snow on the ground and many boots are in bad condition, I have today distributed the 33 pairs of boots as best I could. The supplying of subsidiary nourishment to 17 recommended cases commenced yesterday.
>
> **14th January 1929**: Another 22 pairs of Sir J. Hinchcliffe boots arrived today and were distributed.
>
> **15th October 1929**: Miss Vera Lingwood M.Sc. gave lessons to top classes on 'Hygiene of Food and drink'.

It might well have gone through the minds of many of her young audience that day that the lecture would have been more suitably entitled: 'Food and Drink — how to get some'.

THE 1920s — PERIOD OF POVERTY

RECORD OF CORPORAL PUNISHMENT

RECORD OF CORPORAL PUNISHMENT

Date.	Name of Scholar.	Age.	Standard or Class.	Nature of the Offence.	Nature and extent of Punishment.	Signature and Grade of Teacher who administered Punishment.	Initials (with date) of Head Teacher
June 4, 1928	E. Burrows	11	V.	Thieving	3 strokes		
Jo " "	Jas Scott	10	V.	"	3 " "		
" 17	R. Hampton	8	IVb	Canteen stephens	2 " "		
" "	J. Todd	"	"	"	4 "		
Jy 3	H. Crump	10	IVb	Motor riding	4 strokes.		
Sep 24	{ J. Nixon, J. Rose, J. Sutton, L. Hickin, R. Hopton, D. Hickin, G. Tarpey, J. Davies, V. Raftis }	8–11	II – VI	Playing in Hut against orders	3 each exc. VP 1 & 6 W		
Sep 29	H. Kitchen	10	IVb	Breach of rule re use of toffee nuts	4 v on feet		
Oct 3	{ R. Ambler, J. Hickey, B. Harrison, H. Hickin, J. Callaghan(?) }	11–13	IV+	Smoking against rule	3 each		
" 7	G. Rowe	9?	ii a	Disobedience & defiance & meditation(?)	3 v.sh		
" 14	J. Yates	11	W	Lying maliciously	(?)		
" 22	W. Kitchen	10	IV.b	Bad lie.	4.		
" 31	J. Gordon	10	IVa	Playing truant	2		
Nov 6	F. Latus	10	IVb	"	3		
" "	J. Boyes	10	Vb	"	3.		

8

Between the Wars
From the School Log

PREVIOUS CHAPTERS have dealt largely with the effect on the school of war, strikes and poverty. Now let us turn chiefly to domestic matters and consider the everyday worries of a headmaster as revealed by the entries in the log book — little accidents, little incidents; problems with staff, parents and pupils; matters of health, some trivial and some grave; and ultimately the first rumblings of renewed war.

> **4th September 1919**: I have today received orders from Dr Wiltshire, the Medical Officer of Health, to exclude all children residing in Albert Street, Carlton Street and Clayton Street, on account of the numerous cases of diphtheria in that district ... The numbers affected are 62 Mixed Department and 62 Infants.
>
> **10th September 1919**: I received a postcard this morning instructing me to close school at noon for half a day on account of Doncaster Races.
>
> **16th September 1919**: Four army huts have been delivered into the school yard today from Moorthorpe Station.
>
> **3rd October 1919**: During this week the country has suffered from a great strike occasioned by the National Union of Railwaymen. The influence has been little felt in school . . . The visit of a circus in South Elmsall also made no appreciable difference to the attendance.
>
> **22nd October 1919**: Mr I. Mc----, 11, King Street, brought three Roman Catholic children to school this morning and asked me to

admit them. The priest, Rev. T. McNiff, afterwards came and asked me to refuse them, on the grounds that change of school was sought on a matter of discipline. I have submitted the case to Wakefield.

27th October 1919: I have received instructions from Wakefield to admit Mc----'s children.

29th January 1920: Mrs Sharpe absent owing to stress of weather. She informed me that this is the first time since commencing duty here on 1/5/05 that she has failed to be at duty owing to weather. Her own pony is ill due to accident. She is dependent on other people for conveyance, and today they refused to turn out.

20th February 1920: Dr. Tyrrell called re. mentally defectives.

16th March 1920: Master Stanley Lawson, a pupil of Moorthorpe School, visited this school and gave an exhibition of art before Classes 7 and 9. The visit was greatly appreciated by our boys.

18th March 1920: Master E. Oldfield is absent this afternoon on a visit to Moorthorpe to give an exhibition in drawing in that school.

22nd March 1920: I have received notices this morning re. increases of salaries under the Burnham Scale. The annual rates are as follows: C. Chapman £280 . . . Mrs Sharpe £240 . . . Mrs Thornton £200 . . . Mrs Marlowe £150 . . .

30th April 1920: Children ran off preliminary heats in connection with May Day Sports. Sweets, provided by a Committee under the auspices of the local Labour Party, were distributed to each child today.

5th May 1920: Miss Benson, Directress of Physical Training, paid a visit to the school.

17th May 1920: Miss Jamieson, Directress of Needlework, attended in the afternoon.

8th September 1920: Schools closed for the day. This holiday given on Leger Day is the extra day granted by the W.R.C.C. as

BETWEEN THE WARS

a reward for work done in the schools on behalf of War Savings Association.

9th December 1920: Owing to the low pressure of gas and resultant bad lighting, the school assembled at 1.15 today and will close at 3.45. This will continue till the Xmas holidays.

18th February 1921: Owing to a visit of Wombwell & Bostock's Menagerie to South Elmsall today, the schools assembled at 1 p.m. and closed at 3.15.

14th April 1921: The lessons have been slightly interrupted this morning to give each child an opportunity of observing an exceptionally fine eclipse of the sun, which lasted from 8.35 to 10.30.

16th January 1922: There has been a heavy snowstorm during the weekend and the roads this morning are impassable for traffic. Mr Chapman arrived by road at 9.50, after having experienced a breakdown. Mrs Sharpe arrived at 10.15, having been obliged to hire a special conveyance from Brierley. Mrs Watson absent all day, no buses running from Shafton.

28th February 1922: Schools closed for the day in honour of the wedding between Princess Mary and Viscount Lascelles.

26th May 1922: Attendance very poor owing to attendance officer's absence from duty.

13th July 1922: Schools closed today for annual school trip – this year to Bridlington.

29th August 1922: A boy (G. Taylor) was brought to me with a small splinter in his posterior due to sliding on the desk seat.

20th October 1922: The premises are to be used by the Church members for the purpose of a Bazaar.

6th February 1923: I have today notified Wakefield of a leaking boiler, also of being without sawdust.

26th April 1923: Schools closed today in honour of Royal Wedding between H.R.H. Duke of York and Lady Elizabeth Bowes-Lyon.

THE NORTHFIELD LOG

8th June 1923: Four new cricket bats have been purchased this week at a cost of £2.12s.

10th July 1923: Annual Scholars' Trip took place last Friday, July 6th. 338 children with many parents journeyed by train to Cleethorpes. The weather was ideal and the trip was successful in every way. There has been a heavy downpour of rain since 5 this morning. The rain was particularly heavy between 8 and 9 a.m. The attendance has therefore suffered severely, only 202 children being present out of 501.

8th January 1924: Mr Hawkesworth is absent today under orders from the medical and sanitary authorities. His brother was removed to hospital yesterday under suspicion of suffering from diphtheria. He is to be medically examined at once and if clear will be allowed to resume forthwith.

17th January 1924: Nurse Harrington visited schools.

4th March 1924: The school will be used tonight for a Whist Drive and Dance to raise funds for the School Sports.

28th April 1924: Mrs Wass absent under orders from Medical Officer of Health, her boy having been removed to hospital suffering from Scarlet Fever.

16th May 1924: A tea attended by combined staffs and members of football team held today to celebrate winning of the Clinic Cup.

23rd May 1924: Mrs Wass absent today owing to infection in home, her daughter Miriam having been taken to hospital suffering from Scarlet Fever.

25th August 1924: Schools re-opened. They have been beautified internally and externally by Mr Partridge of South Kirkby.

26th August 1924: Mr G.E. Burton, Temperance Lecturer, gave a lecture to 180 boys of Standards 4, 5, 6 and 7 in the Central Hall. The lecture lasted from 1.45 to 2.45, was ably given and much appreciated.

27th August 1924: Mr Burton repeated his Lecture on Temperance in its relationship with Health to 48 girls of

Standard 4 and 110 girls of Standards 4, 5, 6 and 7 from the Senior Girls' Department.

4th September 1924: P.C. Cockerill visited the school re. a £1 Treasury Note reported to have been found by Edward B---.

15th September 1924: The found Treasury Note handed to Mr B—.

25th September 1924: I have removed Edward B--- from the Register, having learned from a press cutting that he has been ordered by the Wakefield magistrates to a reformatory for six years under a charge of 'found wandering'.

28th October 1924: Polling booths erected in hall.

29th October 1924: General Election — school closed.

20th November 1924: Internal Exam of County Minor Scholarship held.

24th November 1924: Opening of Education Week. Handbills circulated to each house in the district.

26th November 1924: 'Open Day' from 10 a.m. to 4 p.m.

28th November 1924: 'Education Week' closes with an Education Meeting at the Miners' Institute, Moorthorpe. Principal speaker J. Chuter Ede, ex M.P.

22nd July 1925: Fire Drill Practice — time 45 seconds.

1st September 1925: A branch of the Village Circulating Library was commenced here last night. 161 books were supplied. 72 were issued on the first night.

7th September 1925: The attendance this morning has been slightly affected by an excursion to Belle View for a Band Contest in which Frickley Band takes part.

15th December 1925: The ground today is covered with snow and the yard contains some delightful slides. Physical Training lessons in Standards 5 to 8 have taken the form of organised sliding with teacher . . . Eight boys from Standards 7 and 8 have joined a class of girls to attend Hemsworth Hippodrome to witness Shakespeare's 'Twelfth Night', played by Hemsworth Secondary School children.

8th February 1926: Messrs. Wm. Hanley & Sons, Builders, of Hemsworth, are erecting 5 additional closets in the Girls' Yard.

30th August 1926: The closets of all departments have been converted into individual flush closets. The closets of the Boys' Department are not yet finished. One closet only can be used and I am informed that this will have to suffice for a few days.

16th September 1926: Dentist attends Church Hall and extracts teeth from children attending here.

28th September 1926: Combined Staffs went for an outing by motor bus to York and Selby. It was a delightful outing.

27th February 1927: Mr McAlister, Sanitary Inspector, visited the school re. low attendance, which is 65% Girls, 74.4% Boys.

24th May 1927: 'Empire Day' Demonstration in Cricket Field by Infants' Department.

30th June 1927: The schools closed at noon for some sports at South Elmsall organised by the Co-operative Societies.

1st July 1927: The schools are closed today for Annual School Trip to Cleethorpes. Owing to the poor prospect of selling sufficient railway tickets to make up the guaranteed number, a guaranteed excursion train was cancelled and the journey was made by road. 177 children and 126 adults were conveyed by 13 motor buses at a charge of 5*s*. 6*d*. adults and 3*s*. 8*d*. children – it being a condition that three children shall occupy two adult seats and that there shall be no overcrowding. The outing was successful in every way.

6th September 1927: Schools closed again for three days for Doncaster Races.

11th November 1927: Remembrance Day. Two minutes' silence observed in classrooms and not in playground as in former years.

8th March 1928: Children taken at 2.50 p.m. to witness Procession presented by Tradesmen in connection with

BETWEEN THE WARS

Shopping Week. School dismissed at 3.45 to enable all to attend Comic Football Match at Moorthorpe.

4th May 1928: I have been absent all week owing to wounds and concussion resulting from a fall from a motor bus.

15th June 1928: I have spent the main portion of this week in examining all the classes in the three R's. Results very poor. Records to be kept.

1st October 1928: Fire drill — 53 seconds.

19th October 1928: I have been suffering for three weeks from a carbuncle on my neck. It has considerably drained my strength. I go tomorrow to Colwyn Bay for a few days' change under doctor's orders.

24th October 1928: Resumed after two days' absence.
Mr Chapman has been in charge.

12th November 1929: Mr Crossley called re. worn-out readers.

3rd March 1930: On Saturday last Mr Chapman summoned Kate H--- for assault and I summoned Harry H--- for threat. In my case the man was bound over and Mr Chapman's case is withdrawn on account of the woman being unable to be present.

14th May 1930: I have today excluded E. Blakey, A. Cunningham and L. Boyer on instructions from Mr. McAlister, Sanitary Inspector, as they are contacts of a known smallpox case.

16th May 1930: Three boys from this school have been chosen for a week's residence at Staithes Camp, near Whitby.

1st September 1930: Three girls recommended for Staithes Camp have been medically examined at Moorthorpe School.

1st September 1930: Report by Mr A.N.G. Peters, H.M.I. Inspected on 9th and 10th July 1930.

'This department reverted again to the mixed type some two years ago, when more than half the boys then in attendance were transferred elsewhere . . . The teaching everywhere is sympathetic and there is evident desire for improvement . . . The district tendency towards unpunctuality is fairly successfully held in check but it is nevertheless regrettable that apparently it cannot be eradicated altogether, and that in matters of personal cleanliness and neatness some of the children are unsatisfactory.

'In the main the work is planned and carried out on traditional lines, with the result that there is very little in the way of advanced instruction. The premises afford no facilities for Handicrafts, Domestic Subjects and Science. For the first two, children are accommodated at a school some distance away . . .

'Emphasis is very wisely laid upon soundness in the fundamental subjects, but here as elsewhere achievement falls considerably short of the objective, partly owing to circumstances for which the staff is not responsible, partly to lack of co-ordinated preparation, teaching and revision, and partly to the fact that many scholars fail to do the best of which they are capable.'

10th October 1930: This has been Health Week. Suitable talks on Health have been given to the Top Classes. As these were given as Citizenship lessons, there was no dislocation of timetable.

28th November 1930: I am advised to enter a nursing home tomorrow to be operated on on Sunday. As my absence may be of some weeks' duration, I am making arrangements for the work to be carried out under Mr Chapman, Head Assistant.

15th January 1931: Resumed duties today.

20th January 1931: Mr. Williamson absent from duty p.m.

3rd March 1931: A Fire Drill practice was given this afternoon and criticism given to each class teacher with a recommendation of such forming the basis of the next Citizenship lesson. Time taken to clear the school 2½ minutes.

1st April 1931: Mr. F. Williamson passed away at 9.45 p.m. yesterday March 31st, after suffering from cancer on the liver since 1st December 1930.

2nd April 1931: The school assembled at 1 p.m. and closed at 3 p.m. without any break to allow the staff to attend the funeral service of the late Headmaster.

1st July 1931: Douglas Williamson sent home with splinter in his leg from desk seat.

BETWEEN THE WARS

9th July 1931: Mr. Swinbank visited school today with a team of boys who gave displays of folk dancing.

24th August 1931: John Swinbank commenced duty as Headmaster today.

6th July 1932: Children's Day, Roundhay Park, Leeds, July 2nd. Children from this school competed in four classes of the Folk Dance Competition and were awarded a First Class Certificate in each. They were placed first in one class and second in another, thus winning prizes to the value of £4.10s.

27th February 1933: Severe wintry conditions prevail. Snow is deep and there is no doubt that this is the cause of the very poor attendance this morning.

28th February 1933: Owing to the thaw, the conditions under foot are even worse than yesterday. The attendance is better but is still bad. Northfield Lane is in a deplorable condition — slush just outside the school gates being 8 or 10 inches deep. It appears to be nobody's business to attend to it. The Head and a few youths made channels in the lane to drain the melting snow, the slush being almost impassable in places for children not well shod.

8th-11th May 1933: Medical Inspection of children born in 1925 and those who have not been examined when between 7 and 8 by Dr. Cairns, Senior Medical Inspector.

1st July 1933: At Roundhay Park, Leeds, the children from this school won two prizes for first, a second and a third in the Folk Dance Competition.

1st November 1934: Mr. A.R--- commenced duty here. An exchange has been made: Mr. R--- of South Elmsall Broad Lane School has been sent here and Mr Evans sent there in his place.

16th January 1935: Immunisation of 213 children this morning.

28th January 1935: Diphtheria immunisation treatment for second time.

18th February 1935: Mr. R---'s unseemly conduct reported to Education Authority.

20th February 1935: Mr. R--- ill-used James T--- this morning. Mother came to school in the afternoon and complained of Mr. R---'s severe treatment of her son James, who she said bore several marks of Mr. R---'s rough handling of the boy.

22nd February 1935: Third visit of the doctor for protective treatment against diphtheria.

26th February 1935: Mr. R--- left school before all the classes were dismissed — seen disappear by lady teachers.

27th February 1935: School nurse interviewed Sidney W--- respecting severe punishment he had just received from Mr. R--- at morning playtime.

15th March, 1935: Sidney W---'s attendance cancelled. He went home at playtime after being punished by Mr. R---.

20th March 1935: Mr. Hoare, the Committee's Organiser of Physical Training, visited the school this afternoon and wished to see the lessons in Physical Training as they appeared on the timetable. I asked Mr. R--- to take his class for physical in the boys' playground at 2.30 for Mr. Hoare to observe. Mr. R--- did not go into the playground as instructed, nor did he attempt to take the physical exercise lesson indoors. I have reported this insubordination and non-adherence to the timetable.

27th March 1935: I went into Mr. R---'s classroom at 2.45 and found his class writing corrections instead of doing physical exercise.

28th March 1935: Mrs S--- visited the school this morning at 9.30. She brought her daughter Vera with her to show me Vera's septic thumb, which she stated was the result of Mr. R--- punishing her on the hand with a ruler. She wished to see the teacher and the ruler but Mr. R--- refused. Vera is under the care of the doctor. Mrs. S--- complained of Mr. R---'s offensive manners . . . Mr. R--- took corrections instead of P.E. without informing Head of the change.

3rd April 1935: Informed Mr. R--- in writing of his offensive practice of expectorating behind the radiator and in the waste paper basket.

8th April 1935: Investigation into Mr. R---'s conduct.

BETWEEN THE WARS 65

18th April 1935: Received a copy of letter sent to Mr. R--- suspending him from duty as Assistant Teacher on the staff of this school from 17th April 1935.

28th January 1936: School closed – Funeral of King George V.

25th February 1936: South Kirkby Council School. Report by Mr. S. Taylor H.M.I. Inspected on various dates in December 1935.

'This is a three-stream Junior Mixed School with more than average efficiency in attainments as well as in tone and discipline. There is initiative in instruction, and spontaneity of response is steadily and persistently cultivated. Both men and women teachers appear to enjoy their work and spare no pains to make it really successful.

'Art and Handwork (including Needlecraft), however, fall well below this general level of the school training and should be carefully overhauled. Few contacts have been made between the classes or the activities themselves. It is because of this lack of purpose and progression that so little is achieved in this important side of the school training.

'Until this section of the school work is established on a level with the rest of the school activities, regular staff conferences should be held for full discussion and criticism of aims, procedure and results.'

17th August 1936: Installation of electric light commenced during the holidays.

14th December 1936: The 3A Class attended the Hemsworth Grammar School Play, 'Crossings', by Walter de la Mare, this afternoon by permission.

22nd January 1937: The attendance this week has been even worse than last week, only 52%, owing to an epidemic of 'flu'. School closed for one week by order of the Medical Officer of Health.

30th January 1937: The Medical Officer of Health extended the period of closure for this school and it is not to open until 15th February 1937.

19th April 1937: Coronation boots were distributed.

6th May 1937: About fifty children were withdrawn from school

THE NORTHFIELD LOG

as permitted by the Education for religious observance of Ascension Day, written notice being given by the parents.

16th August 1937: Derek B--- has been awarded the Holgate Scholarship providing complete exemption from payment of tuition fees and a maintenance allowance of £10 a year.

2nd December 1937: The dentist was 'smoked out' of the male teachers' room, which he is using for dental treatment of the children.

3rd December 1937: The dentist found it impossible to do his work again today, owing to smoking chimney and room full of soot.

7th December 1937: Dr. Cairns, Senior Medical Officer, visited the school to examine the children. He recommended several children for two bottles of milk daily.

14th January 1938: Treat for the Children of the Unemployed.

9th January 1939: The damp walls and the clammy atmosphere of the school make it unfit for the children and teachers to be in.

14th February 1939: Boys' Gatepost badly damaged by scavengers' motor.

22nd March 1939: The County Medical Officer inspected all the children present and recommended subsidiary nourishment for many.

10th May 1939: Representative of Board of Education, County Education Dept., called concerning A.R.P. (Air Raid Precautions) Trenches.

23rd October 1939: Visit of Mr. Ecclestone, County Council Inspector and a representative of the Board, to discuss the proposals for the commencement of a war emergency garden at this school.

25th October 1939: Visit of the Authority's representatives in connection with the siting of trenches.

BETWEEN THE WARS 67

Northfield school reports dated 1929 and 1930 .....

Form 195.
Head Teacher's Report

COUNTY COUNCIL OF THE WEST RIDING OF YORKSHIRE.

EDUCATION DEPARTMENT.

.... South Kirkby C.E. .... SCHOOL. ...Mixed... DEPT

SCHOLAR'S REPORT for... half..... year ..... ended ......31. 3. ...... 193 0

Name ...... Lawrence H. ...... Class 8., Std IIIA.

Parents are requested to examine carefully the following Report, so that the Children may be encouraged to take interest in their work at School.

SUBJECT.	MARKS.	REMARKS ON SUBJECT.
Reading	6	Fair.
Writing	8	Good. Very round & neat.
Arithmetic	5	Fair. Sometimes one of the best.
English		
(a) Composition	6	Fair. This is improving now.
(b) Grammar		
(c) Spelling	5	Rather on the weak side yet.
(d) Recitation	4½	Shows a rather bad memory for poems.
History	7	Good. Lawrie remembers
Geography	7	these subjects better.
Nature Study and Lessons on Common Things	8	
Drawing	7	Good. One of the best at times.
Handwork	7	Good.
Needlework		
Special Subjects (if any)		
Mental Arith.	7	Good
Scripture	6	Fair

Attendances Possible... 218   Position in Class... 20th
Times Absent... 16   Number in Class... 53
Times Late... 1   Average Age of Class... 8 y 11 m

Explanation of Marks: E.—Excellent; V.G.—Very Good; G.—Good; F.G.—Fairly Good; F.—Fair; B.—Bad or Fail.

CONDUCT AND GENERAL REMARKS. Lawrence is moving nicely in most subjects, though he has not yet quite recovered the ground lost through illness in the first term - as a rule he is interested & well behaved, but occasionally he is inattentive & allows his mind to wander.

.... F. Williamson Head Teacher.
.... E Hutt Class Teacher.

..... The class teacher, E. Hutt, was the author's aunt.

9

The Second World War

Whistle while you work . . .
Hitler is a twerp . . .

Hitler, you are barmy,
You want to join the army . . .

THE ABOVE VERSES are not to be found in the Northfield log book. They come from the depths of my own distant memory. The first intimation from the log of the impending cataclysm is, as recorded at the end of the previous chapter, a note about a visit from a representative of the Education Authority, dated 10th May, regarding the siting of trenches.

As in 1914, the school was on holiday the day war was declared. On 1st September 1939 Germany invaded Poland, and two days later Britain declared war on Germany. When school re-opened on 11th September after the summer break, life continued as if nothing had happened. No further hint occurred until, on 23rd October, there was a reference to the setting up of a war emergency garden. It is worth bearing in mind, however, that the headmaster, John Swinbank, made relatively sparse use of the log book compared with his predecessor, making a mere eight entries all told between September and Christmas 1939.

Following up the Authority's directives, air-raid shelters were situated beneath the small field in front of the school — the sealed cavity remains to this day — and a war emergency garden was established and carefully nurtured, creating a splendid addition to the curriculum. It was anticipated in 1939 — quite correctly — that foodstuffs would become extremely difficult to import from overseas because of enemy action at sea, and that a system of rationing would eventually be needed. Therefore, the need was stressed for people to develop the habit of cultivating their own food in their own gardens and allotments. To that end, the school's war emergency garden was a valuable and productive exercise, and in this way Northfield played its part in the widely publicized 'Dig for Victory' campaign.

Because of the wartime emergency and its repercussions upon each household, the summer holiday of 1940 was somewhat different from normal:

> **22nd July 1940**: School to remain open for the next four weeks. Attendance recommended but not compulsory.

Unfortunately the attendance figures for this particular period are not recorded!

On 9th September Joseph Thorpe, who had joined the staff in 1938, left school for military service, returning safely in April 1946. The arrival of his replacement is recorded on 14th October 1940:

> Miss Marjorie Atkins, evacuee from the Channel Islands, commenced duty here this morning.

Contingency plans for the evacuation of children living in the cities had been made several months before war broke out. At the beginning of September 1939 about 1½ million were evacuated to country areas. Partly because of the absence of air-raids that autumn, and partly because so many evacuees could not adapt to country life, nearly three quarters of them had returned to their home cities by Christmas, preferring to risk the eventual coming of the air-raids, rather than endure the dull – though comparatively safe – rural existence. The Channel Islands, with their close proximity to occupied France, were in grave danger. In 1940 they were swiftly overrun by the Germans – and Miss Atkins, who had taught at Asherst Girls' School in Guernsey up to the time of her evacuation, was forced to remain in South Kirkby until the end of August 1945.

THE SECOND WORLD WAR 71

No other mention of evacuees is made in the log, apart from the names of five girls and one boy, who are listed in August 1943: 'Philip West, Rosemary and Gwendoline Cose (?), Gladys Bradford, Brenda Paul, Maureen Baldwin.' There is no mention of whereabouts they came from, where they stayed or for how long.

Very little of the war-time atmosphere is conveyed by the log. Swinbank's record is far more trite, far less enlightening, than Williamson's had been. Indeed, during the First World War years from 1914 to 1918 Williamson filled sixty-two pages of the log. Between 1939 and 1945, Swinbank took up a mere nineteen pages, most of them with staff lists and annual lists of successful County Minor Scholarship candidates. 'Salute the Soldier' week, in May 1944, merits the briefest possible mention, yet this was a most exciting event for Northfield children, an occasion of great patriotic fervour, when little boys were dressed up in navy, army and air-force uniforms, and little girls proudly paraded in nurses' uniforms.

On 8th May 1945 there was dancing, and there were parties in the streets. Victory in Europe was celebrated with wild enthusiasm and unrestrained joy. The log book records the landmark in the following words:

8th-9th May 1945: V.E. Days — school closed.

'Salute the Soldier' week at Northfield, May 1944

10

Improving Northfield's Image

SWINBANK RETIRED as Head in August 1947, to be succeeded by Donald Gordon. In the aftermath of war the school was demoralized, overcrowded and ill-equipped. Over the next few years Gordon was to set it on the road to recovery, to such an extent that it became something of a show school.

A keen interest in the local environment was at once encouraged. This new enthusiasm resulted in the pupils being taken out of school on educational visits on an unprecedented scale. Environmental studies or, to quote from the log entry dated 8th July 1947, 'work based on a centre of interest', took classes to such places as Musgrave's (a local 'bus garage), an un-named instrument factory in the village, South Elmsall gas-works, and the Mexborough based printing works of the *South Yorkshire Times*, in connection with the children's 'Top Class Times' newspaper project.

As well as creating links between school and local industry, an interest in local history was pursued:

> **7th September 1949**: Mr Chapman took his class to visit site of Saxon Camp.

The clearly-defined earthworks of this encampment, established by the Ancient Britons and later occupied by the Saxons, lies on the slopes of Brierley Common, just outside South Kirkby.

Another local project had been carried out the previous year, when a class of students had been escorted to the nearby village of Hooton Pagnell to visit Hooton Pagnell Hall (a medieval building with a well-preserved fourteenth century gatehouse), the home of the local land-owning Warde-Aldam family.

The nearest historical site to the school, and probably the most frequently visited, was All Saints Church, a mere two minute walk from Northfield. The church dates back to 1131, but the original stone building collapsed during a storm in 1470 and was then virtually rebuilt. One of the chief sources of interest inside the church is its furniture, the installation of some of which was recorded in the log on 21st January 1953:

> Mr Chapman took his class to visit the Church, where the famous Thompson firm were putting in new pews.

The carpentry firm of Robert Thompson, who was born in 1876, was established in the North Yorkshire village of Kilburn. When he was twenty he joined his father (who was a joiner, carpenter and wheelwright), and the firm began to specialize in the making of furniture, with a special emphasis on church furniture. Hewn from solid oak by means of an adze rather than a plane, each piece carries the Thompson trademark: a little mouse, first created in 1925 and chosen to represent 'Industry in quiet places'. South Kirkby Church is full of mice − on the choir screen, on candlesticks, on a lectern − but, most prolific of all, on the pews. Since 1953 scores of children have hunted excitedly for them.

The nature of school excursions became more and more ambitious. Between 1948 and 1953, full day outings were organized to Hull (three times), Conisbrough and Doncaster, Harewood House, Fountains Abbey and Stump Cross Caverns, Spurn Point, Ripon and the Washburn Valley, the Lake District and the Peak District. The annual trip to the seaside was gone, to be replaced by a curriculum-based coach excursion. One particular visit instigated by Gordon showed his determination to improve the school's image. Money for basic improvements, such as indoor toilets and civilized dining facilities, was impossible to come by as yet, but at least something might be done to make the exterior of the place look more attractive. Consequently the following trip was arranged:

> **22nd September 1949**: . . . a visit to Ackworth Stone Quarry, in connection with work on rockery.

Soon afterwards further environmental improvements were noted:

> **20th February 1950**: Trees planted along the front of school today — three limes and three silver birches.

Later on in the year 21 shrubs and trees, plus planting accessories, were ordered from Backhouse's Nurseries of York, for a cost of £17 10s. 6d. It is recorded that planting took place on 18th December 1950 by children of Class 2.

Another visit, first recorded in April 1948, became a regular feature of the curriculum:

> Instruction in Swimming commenced at Frickley Baths.

These visits continued, on and off, for nearly twenty years, but were confined to the top classes. Swimming instruction on more positive lines was introduced in the late 'Sixties, when the ill-equipped Frickley Baths was replaced by a new building adjacent to the new Minsthorpe High School. Formal instruction then became a compulsory feature of the timetable for the First and Second Year pupils (nine to eleven year olds) of the new Middle Schools.

Gordon organized outings of a cultural nature: to see a stage production of *Oliver Twist* at Doncaster, to see the biographical film *Scott of the Antarctic*, and a trip to Doncaster Art Gallery, all in 1949. The pupils' experience of life was further enriched by a series of visitors. A taste of culture was provided on 4th March 1949 by the West Riding String Quartet. Other notable visitors are recorded in the log as follows:

> **11th July 1952**: Visit of ten students from Lady Mabel College of Physical Education, Wentworth. Children were especially interested in Miss Heather Armitage, the British sprint champion, a member of the party. She left school to fly to Helsinki, Finland, to represent Britain in the Olympic Games there next week.

(Miss Armitage came nowhere in 1952, but took 6th place in the 100 metres at Melbourne in 1956.)

IMPROVING NORTHFIELD'S IMAGE

26th March 1953: Skipper Pearson, to whom Class 1 have written for nearly two years, paid a surprise visit. He is skipper of a Hull trawler, which fishes in northern waters. He boarded and claimed as prize the *Westclaus*, abandoned off Flamborough Head last year, and received a decoration for the exploit.

(On a visit to Hull a few weeks later as guests of Skipper Pearson, Class 1 was taken on a trawler trip and the head records: 'The trawler owners Marr & Co. sent us home with four boxes of fish.')

30th November 1955: The children of Mr Thorpe's class last year had been in continuous correspondence with the Naturalist Trust bird watcher Miss Barbara Whittaker on Lundy. She mentioned the interest of the children to a Mr. Hook of Bournemouth, another naturalist, who offered to come at his own expense to show films he had taken of bird and seal life on the island. He spent the day in school showing films and answering questions.

That aforementioned visit to Doncaster Art Gallery in 1949 reflected Donald Gordon's chief interest in life, and the chief means by which he proceeded to raise the morale of Northfield. The purpose of the visit on that occasion had been to look at the 'West Riding Schools Collection', which was on exhibition there, in the hope that a little enthusiasm would be stirred up in the children's imagination.

He had inherited a run-down, underprivileged establishment, lacking in many basic amenities. While it was likely to be a long time before the school could be granted such essentials as a proper meals service or indoor toilets, or even a telephone, at least he could encourage each class to brighten up the place through art work. Without neglecting other sides of the curriculum, the wider aspects of art were brought into every possible facet of school life.

A report issued by His Majesty's Inspectors following a visit made in November 1950 remarks about the inadequate heating and the congestion in school (among other drawbacks) but comments at length on the efforts to beautify the place, mentioning in particular the 'delightful rockery', the newly planted trees, and the flower boxes. 'These praiseworthy efforts to make the school more attractive have won the respect of the community,' said the report. It continued . . .

THE NORTHFIELD LOG

> The interior of the school is bright and cheerful . . . The appearance of the hall and classrooms shows that Art is playing a prominent part in the life of the school. The boys and girls are having a rich experience of colour and many opportunities for working with a variety of media, including some for three-dimensional work. Patterns are made in all classes, but they are seen at their best in the upper forms where they are applied to a craft . . . not only does the needlework reflect the influence of the art teaching in the school but the recorded work in English, History, Geography and Nature Study does as well.

Before long there was a constant flow of visitors from all over the world, and Gordon's Northfield became firmly established as a show school. The following entries in the log book testify to the success that the school now enjoyed:

> **16th December 1952**: Mr. Rocke and Mr. Field (West Riding Art Advisers) visited and brought with them Mr. Cyril Cross of Leeds College of Art and (at the suggestion of Mr. Clegg, the Chief Education Officer), Mr. Maurice de Sansmarez, lecturer in Fine Art at Leeds University. They came to see Christmas cards done by children in various media.

> **29th September 1953**: Four high-powered German professors of psychology, education and philosophy visited this afternoon, accompanied by Mr. Thornton (Deputy Chief Education Officer).

> **13th April 1954**: 25 German visitors and 15 English teachers visited the school. Mr. Clegg brought Mr. Schiller, H.M.I., Chief of Primary Education, and Mr. de Sansmarez. Mime and movement by Mrs. Gordon was seen and all work examined. Mr. Clegg called all staff together at the conclusion of the day to thank them for the excellent work that had been seen. In the evening the head was invited to Woolley Hall* to answer questions put by the visitors on the various aspects of the work.

> **14th May 1954**: Asked by Mr Cotterill, H.M.I., to select 30 to 40 paintings to send to Ministry of Education, Curzon Street House, London, as a display of the school's work in art.

*At that time Woolley Hall was a teachers' training college; now it is a teachers' advisory centre run by Wakefield M.D.C.

> **6th July 1954**: Mr. Rocke brought two Norwegian visitors to look round school. He took examples of art work for a teachers' course at Mexborough.

In the margin alongside that entry, Gordon pencilled in: '304 visitors since February 1950, not including C.C.I.'s* and H.M.I.'s.'

On 19th July 1954 a letter from the Education Office in Wakefield was pasted into the log book: 'To Head Teachers: There is an Exhibition of work done by pupils at the South Kirkby Primary School in Northfield Lane, South Kirkby, which Mr. Rocke considers to be of a very high standard, and hopes that teachers in the locality who can spare the time will see this work . . .' The exhibition ran for three days and Gordon records that 119 teachers visited, representing over twenty schools within a twelve mile radius.

> **8th March 1955**: Mrs. Rocke and a Javanese lady (from the Java Ministry of Education) visited this afternoon. Art work taken for an exhibition at Sheffield Institute of Education.

> **19th May 1955**: Mr. A.B. Clegg, Chief Education Officer, visited this morning. He brought with him his relative, Mr. Attenborough, father of 'Dicky', the film and radio actor.

Next came a request from the Ministry of Education to send examples of art work to schools in Japan. The Ministry then sent a party of Egyptians to tour Northfield, closely followed by visitors from North America, who took back to Wayne University, Detroit, examples of art-enhanced booklets done by the children. The renowned Dartington Hall School in Devon was represented among the catalogue of visitors in 1958, when the Principal of Further Education and the Art Master looked round the school.

As was noted in the H.M.I.'s report of 1950, the art influence extended to needlework. Gordon was also anxious to diversify into work with clay, for which purpose a kiln was acquired in April 1954. Certain problems had to be overcome, however, before satisfactory results could be achieved:

*County Council Inspectors

23rd June 1954: Mr. Rocke called to enquire into the cause of the delay in fitting the kiln.

24th June 1954: Great activity this afternoon to fit out the small room in the Boys' Porch to house the kiln. Activities directed by Clerk of Works.

25th June 1954: Kiln switched on for first time this afternoon. Results to contents resembled minor atomic explosion. Mr. Chapman absent until 3 p.m. Minor operation at hospital − not due to above.

30th June 1954: Kiln behaving itself as experience of its temperament grows.

There was one particular occasion when it seemed to Gordon that there was actually too much painting going on. The entry for 26th October 1953 reads as follows:

> School reopened after October holiday. The painters had started to decorate the school during the holiday. The Divisional Education Officer said they were to continue during school time; one class at a time had to move into the hall. I protested strongly against the inconvenience and interference with the school programme. D.E.O. said it was an order of the Chief Education Officer Mr. Clegg himself. Mr. Cook, Administrative Assistant, arrived this morning too, and, striding over paint cans, announced that he had been sent by Mr. Clegg to see some of the work in this school before taking over the post of Assistant Director of Education for Liverpool. He saw a lot of painting, both children's and adults'.

Gordon managed to raise Northfield to the status of show school, and yet working conditions for staff and children alike were still depressing. When His Majesty's Inspectors visited in November 1950 a boiler had broken down and the temperature throughout school was a maximum of 48°F. Other comments made concerned the girls' cloakroom − 175 girls had to make do with a room twelve feet square, making hand-washing before lunch particularly difficult. 'It is understood that hot water will soon be available at the hand basins.' Those same girls had to go across the yard to visit the toilet. 'There are only five W.C.'s, and

IMPROVING NORTHFIELD'S IMAGE

three of the pedestals were without wooden rims at the time of inspection.'

The tiny rooms used as headmaster's study and staff room — both about six feet by ten feet — were commented on. Three years later no improvements had been forthcoming. In April of 1953 Gordon listed in the log book defects which were still outstanding:

1. Inadequate heating.
2. No hot water at handbasins.
3. Inadequate number of W.C.'s for girls.
4. Inadequate cloakroom facilities and meals service congestion.
5. Repairs needed to fabric of blocks of lavatories, boundary walls and main building.
6. Still no flushing system for boys' urinals.

A copy of this list was forwarded to the Education Office at Wakefield.

Despite the efforts made to brighten up a deprived school's environment, there must have been a great sense of relief for the children at hometime, when the opportunity came to break free from the cramped, confined and overcrowded building. There was one small recreation ground in the village — just a few swings, a slide and a roundabout — but one of the favourite playgrounds, especially for the boys, was the vast, sprawling, but obviously very dangerous environs of South Kirkby Colliery, whose mountainous spoil-heaps loomed over the school and neighbouring terraces and estates. The log book records several tragic consequences of using such prohibited playgrounds:

> **25th July 1950**: Two boys from Class 1 . . . were drowned in the Colliery Reservoir this evening.
>
> **23rd June 1954**: The tragic death by drowning of T--- C--- (aged 8 years) of Colliery Row was reported this morning. His body was found last evening in the stretch of water near the colliery tips. Head teacher and Miss Heathcote, class teacher, visited the child's home this morning.
>
> **3rd May 1957**: The tragic news that D--- M---, a boy in Class 5, had been electrocuted whilst trespassing on the pit property last evening, was brought to school this morning. Warned all

children in school of the danger of playing in the vicinity of the pit.

The most chaotic part of any school day during Gordon's time was lunch-time. One could hardly expect otherwise in an establishment with no kitchen for the preparation of meals, no dining hall, totally inadequate washing-up facilities and two or three hundred hungry children waiting to be fed. It was way back in 1906 that education authorities were first permitted, via the Education (Provision of Meals) Act of that year, to provide meals for elementary schoolchildren, though there was no compulsion to do so. When it was felt necessary — as, for example, during the Miners' Strike of 1912 — authorities could either work in conjunction with charitable institutions or make provision via the rates, in which case the maximum sum levied was a halfpenny in the pound. Not surprisingly the school meals service was slow to gain favour. Six years after the Act, only about a third of the 322 education authorities in England and Wales were providing the service.

One authority which was pulling its weight was Bradford, where in 1907 a central cooking depot was set up at Green Lane School. Food prepared here was distributed to six school centres in Bradford. A few months later nearly two thousand meals were distributed daily by wagon to thirteen locations. Forty years later it was a scheme similar to the pioneering Bradford scheme which provided Northfield with its first regular school meals service, when the 1944 Education Act decreed that meals and milk must be provided. Meals prepared a mile away at Moorthorpe were distributed to schools throughout the area by van, the cooked food being sealed in metal containers to keep it as hot as possible. Crockery and cutlery were stored in the already congested corridors at Northfield, and washing-up was somehow performed in the cloakrooms. The inspectors who visited in November 1950 described conditions thus:

> About 220 boys and girls stay for the mid-day meal. In addition to the hall, two classrooms have to be used. The boys put up the tables at the morning interval, thus depriving the school of the use of the hall each day from eleven o'clock. The impression

IMPROVING NORTHFIELD'S IMAGE

gained during the eating of the meal is one of eagerness to press matters through as quickly as possible. The crowded conditions, the feeling of hurry and the inadequate cloakroom facilities militate against the efforts of the members of staff to turn the meal into a valuable social occasion. The food itself was palatable and the helpings sufficient.

A spate of log entries in late 1947 illustrates some of the hazards of the school meals system:

> **19th November 1947**: Owing to breakdown in heating supply, school dinners could not be served until about 1.30 p.m. All children were told to go home during dinner period. The meal arrived at 1.50 p.m. and the children were served at once.
>
> **3rd December 1947**: Owing to breakdown in gas supply, the dinners were late. The children were sent home at noon with instructions to get some light refreshment. The meals arrived at 2 p.m. and the children were served immediately.
>
> **4th December 1947**: Owing to the failure of the gas supply again, the canteen supplied sandwiches and ginger pudding for lunch today.
>
> **18th December 1947**: This morning every member of staff complained of having suffered from diarrhoea and sickness during the night. On enquiry it was found that about a third of the children had similar symptoms. Some form of food poisoning was suspected . . .'

Obviously something needed to be done about the entire school dinner procedure. Conditions were reported and investigated. Two years later, in April 1950, a recommendation came from the West Riding School Meals Organizer that a hot-plate, new tables and benches and an electric water geyser be provided. Two years later still, in May 1952, comes the entry:

> Received a letter this morning from Divisional Education Officer regarding washing up equipment. After storing this in school for nearly two years, the Authority find that, on account of limitation of School Meals Capital Expenditure, it is not possible to install it during this financial year. The whole bag of tricks has been collected this morning and returned to West Riding Stores.

Nine days later it is recorded:

> Gas boiler returned by van today — no word of explanation received concerning these comings and goings.

Various plans were put forward. In 1953 a new canteen was projected; this was swiftly scrapped, because it would take too much light away from certain classrooms, and in any case the Managers had decided at their last meeting to recommend the building of a new junior school. In 1954 it was suggested '. . . that the present miniature staffroom be converted into a canteen scullery and a new staffroom be provided.' Also in 1954 an H.M.I. recommendation was put forward, suggesting that a dining hall with scullery attached be built at an estimated cost of £3,500. This was turned down two years later 'owing to lack of funds.'

The problems of overcrowding were ever prevalent. In the Junior department there were nine classrooms to accommodate 350 pupils. In 1953 permission was granted to create a tenth class, to be based in the Northfield Methodist Chapel Schoolroom — precisely where the school had been born fifty years earlier. The school continued to burst at the seams. In September 1955 two prefabricated rooms were erected on the school field. The number of pupils on roll continued to rise, and as late as 1964 a second class had to be housed in the chapel, this time in its tiny kitchen.

In 1959 Donald Gordon left to take up a similar post in a totally dissimilar location — Harrogate. Under the leadership of the new head, John Glover, Northfield maintained a high academic standard amid low standards of accommodation. Proposals continued to be made, and to be rejected — as, for example, the following:

> **26th March 1963**: Visited by architects from the West Riding Architects' Department, to discuss the provision of indoor toilets for the children. The position is not encouraging, as no suitable place could be found in the existing building.

Then, following visits in the winter and spring of 1963, a report by Her Majesty's Inspectors started a ball rolling. The class in the chapel was mentioned. So was the regular lunchtime chaos, with particular emphasis laid upon the one small sink for washing up after serving 300 meals. A site where the junior school and its neighbouring infants' department, containing over 700 pupils, still had no telephone, must have caused the inspecting team some astonishment as well as alarm. The social and general training of the children was highly praised. Despite the grimness of its environment and the hardships endured by its staff and pupils, the report declared, 'It is a happy school to be in.'

Shortly afterwards, on 27th January 1964, it was recorded: 'Headmaster attended meeting at Wakefield to discuss rehabilitation plans for this school. It is proposed to spend about £28,000 on canteen, dining hall and indoor toilets over the next three years.'

In September of that year a new infants' school, Burntwood, was opened in South Kirkby. The subject of Comprehensive Education was mentioned for the first time. Meetings were held to gain teachers' support for a new experimental division of children into Primary Schools for 5 to 9 years, Middle Schools for 9 to 13, and High Schools for 13 plus, and in the process doing away with the 'Eleven Plus'.

In April 1965 it was confirmed that Northfield was to be converted into a Middle School. Two months later, work began at last on the rehabilitation programme. At the beginning of 1966, demolition work took place on the infamous outdoor toilets. About this time it was revealed that, following the abolition of the 'Eleven Plus', Comprehensive reorganization would commence in September 1968. The local Hemsworth Grammar School would become Hemsworth High School, and a new high school would be built at Minsthorpe for the South Elmsall, South Kirkby and Upton area.

At the beginning of 1967 the new canteen was ready for use. For the first time in its sixty year existence, Northfield was able to provide suitable dining facilities for its pupils. The new dining hall, adjacent to the canteen, also contained exciting new gymnasium equipment, and there was adequate space for a daily assembly for the whole school, a venture which hitherto had been impracticable. However, as the hall contained a large proportion of glass, it had the qualities of a greenhouse. A warm and sunny June regularly produced temperatures in excess of 100°F. The

remedy was new curtains, which were hung in May 1968.
On 18th September 1967, John Glover recorded in the log:

> There are no workmen in school today. It would appear that, after 2½ years of unspeakable disorder and inconvenience, the rehabilitation programme is at last complete.

A year later, on 9th September 1968, Northfield finally changed its title from Junior Mixed and Infants to Northfield Middle School and became one of the first middle schools in the country.

Apart from the hall and canteen, little else was actually new. With no infants on site any more, some of their redundant classrooms and their old assembly hall were converted into toilets, staffroom and — another novelty — secretary's office. Although it was a luxury for the children to have indoor toilets, it was unfortunate that further alterations could not have been included to allow for showers and adequate changing facilities for twelve and thirteen year old boys and girls. An old school had been knocked about to create an illusion of something new, under a new name and with new educational concepts to pursue. Life still went on within an antiquated shell, but the splendid new meals service, the indoor toilets and the gymnasium facilities were greatly appreciated. What was appreciated most of all, though, was the sense of space which Northfield had never before experienced. Less than 400 children now occupied the site where not long before nearly twice as many had been uncomfortably crammed. For the first time ever, the children of Northfield had room to sit and work, to play and run, to grow and learn in comfort.

J.T. Glover, Head of Northfield 1959-1977
(Portrait by Sherilyn Hutt)

IMPROVING NORTHFIELD'S IMAGE 85

May Day at Northfield, 1947

Northfield in the late 1950s

86   THE NORTHFIELD LOG

Fourth Year class, 1963

Staff group, 1965. John Glover, headmaster, is in the centre of front row.
Peter Nuttall, the present head, is immediately behind him.

11

John Thomas Glover

JOHN GLOVER was born during the First World War in the village of Thurnscoe, an area of deprivation very similar to South Kirkby. He spent most of the Second World War serving in the Persian Desert, and in later years never tired of relating his experiences in the staff-room. He took up teaching after the war and, prior to becoming head of Northfield, he had been a deputy head in Hemsworth for a number of years.

His early days at Northfield were fraught with difficulties. His predecessor, Donald Gordon, had built up a loyal and experienced staff, many of whom expressed their disappointment at his departure by quitting with him or as soon as possible after him. There was a serious national shortage of qualified teachers in the early 'Sixties. Consequently, Glover's problems in successfully taking over the reins from Gordon were manifold. He commenced duty at Northfield in September 1959; in 1961 there were still two students fresh from grammar school, and three itinerant supply teachers, on the staff of twelve. Not until 1968 did he achieve a full complement of qualified and experienced teachers, three of whom are still at Northfield.

He developed a great pride in his school, its pupils and its staff. He expected loyalty and a caring attitude, and in return he was a courteous and considerate leader, highly respected by everyone with whom he came into contact. When an irate mother threatened to attack a member of staff with a badminton racquet, for chastising her rumbustious son, he was on hand to pacify the lady. When another member of staff devised a local studies project which involved an innocuous home questionnaire, a parent took this as an unwarranted invasion of privacy and reported the matter to the press. Once again, with a minimum of fuss, Glover stepped in to defuse the potentially explosive situation.

Such matters, however, failed to reach the log book, which now began to develop a formal diary style, consisting chiefly of the recording of staff absences, of accidents to pupils, and of visits and visitors.

There are two incidents recorded in the log, however, which reflect the pride he took in Northfield. It was very much his school, and the staff who helped him run the place on well-oiled lines had, to a large extent, been nurtured by his own personal influence. He resented what he considered to be any unwarranted intrusion. For example, in October 1973 he was dismayed when the school governors overruled him on a matter of outside organizations being permitted to use the school premises: 'The local Boys' Brigade have been granted permission to make use of our school hall on Tuesday evenings.' He managed to veil his own personal feelings in that particular entry, but a few weeks later there was perhaps less effort taken to disguise what he really felt about a scheme which had been carried out on the school premises during the summer holidays:

> **17th October 1973**: There was a meeting of Governors, Play Group Leaders and Council representatives to talk about holiday play groups. It was a most unpleasant meeting.

His efforts to maintain the status quo at Northfield sometimes went to extraordinary lengths. Whenever a member of staff was about to be married, there was inevitably a heart-to-heart chat, in which Glover would make a conscious effort to persuade the other to think twice before taking such an irrevocable step. Though happily married himself, he held a rather cynical view of marriage. In the case of the Northfield staff, however, he simply did not want to lose his lady teachers to the chores of raising families, or allow his male members of staff to get ideas about taking their wives and families to other more attractive parts of the country in search of promotion. Every member of his team was hand-picked, was his protégé, and was a reflection of the pride he took in Northfield.

JOHN THOMAS GLOVER 89

Fourth Year Class, 1967, the last year of Northfield Lane Junior Mixed

John Glover's Middle School staff, 1971, five of whom are still there.

Two views of Northfield, 1967

12

Northfield Middle School

HAVING MOULDED the Northfield staff more or less to his own specifications and endured the transitional period from Junior to Middle School, as well as the difficult rebuilding programme, Glover's rôle now was to provide a secure footing for this experimental phase of education in South Kirkby. A purpose-built middle school was established in nearby Grimethorpe, under the headship of Tom Gannon, who was later rewarded at Buckingham Palace for his services. Glover's task was far harder. He did not have the luxury of a new school, with every conceivable amenity. He had to advertise the new educational system and make it work within the framework of an old school, whose conversion to modernity was only partially successful.

The first day of 'Northfield County Middle School' – the 'County' was dropped shortly afterwards – was scheduled for 9th September 1968. There would be 305 on roll at the commencement, with a 2½ form entry and a staff consisting of head, deputy head and ten assistant teachers. This would be the first year with an extended age group up to twelve. In the following September the top age would be raised to thirteen, by which time the new system would be fully functional – from age nine to age thirteen.

In order that every member of staff – and the head himself – might be as fully prepared as possible to deal with the unknown at the beginning of the new academic year, an extraordinary staff meeting was convened on 29th July 1968 and occupied several hours on both that evening and on the next. The minutes were recorded in ten typewritten sheets, and pasted into the log book.

Glover began by stating that:

> The school will be divided into four teaching units (one for each year of children), and a team of teachers will be allocated to each unit. Each teaching unit will have its classrooms and a Shared Area, which will contain the shared library and the shared apparatus and equipment. The degree of teacher co-operation within a teaching unit must be high.

For most of the staff, team teaching was to be a novel experience. The degree of staff co-operation formerly required had been slight. I had been teaching at Northfield for five years and had had my own class of thirty or forty ten and eleven year old 'B' children from nine till four every day, only relinquishing them to another staff member for a twice-weekly music lesson. At that time, conditions were largely governed by intensive 'Eleven Plus' drilling for those 'A' children considered to be in with a chance of making the selection for grammar school. Now, the pupils in my charge were of all abilities, and I was to work in close liaison with at least one other member of staff. My new working area consisted of two classrooms separated by a space, which had been converted from a classroom into the so-called shared area, with an open archway connecting with the classroom on each side.

With the abolition of grammar schools and the introduction of the comprehensive system, permanent streaming was no longer considered to be a necessity. As Glover explained in his extensive notes, under the new system ...

> ... each year of children will be put into small groups (about ten children) according to ability. The groups will be mixed sexes. For different types of work, these small groups will join together in different ways. There will be times when it is better to have the abler groups working together, and times when mixing the abilities is advantageous.

He expressed the hope that with this system of 'Bi-lateral Grouping' the advantages of both streamed and unstreamed teaching would be achieved. Streaming was to be retained for maths and English, and the newly-introduced subject of French was to commence with streamed classes. Such subjects as history, geography and science were bracketed under the title 'Humanities', and were to be treated with a non-streamed approach.

The proposed breakaway from the old class-bound tradition of the primary school was further emphasized by Glover's remark that:

> The teaching of specialist subjects such as Music, French and Religious Instruction may require the services of teachers outside a particular teaching unit. Thus an exchange of time between teachers of different years will be desirable.

However, the sort of specialization which had prevailed in the secondary schools would have no place in Glover's middle school.

> No middle school teacher will teach only one or two subjects all day. The middle school teacher will provide for most of the needs of the children in his care, but will be given the opportunities to spend more time on the subject or subjects in which he is particularly interested. No individual teacher will be a teacher of 'A' stream children or 'B' stream children. All will be concerned in the teaching of the whole group.

More innovations were the idea of a daily 'free choice' period, 'when they can pursue some interest of the moment,' and 'Integrated Teaching', when the normal timetable could be temporarily suspended to allow 'Art, Craft, English, Maths and any other subject to be related to a topic.'

One more subject which merited special attention at the staff meeting was physical education. The extension of Northfield's age-range from eleven to thirteen created certain sensitivities which the staff had not experienced before. Should the senior children be segregated or in mixed classes? How should the problem of changing facilities be dealt with in a school where there were none? With the assurance that 'It is hoped to provide changing rooms in the near future,' Glover reported the decision that:

> For the time being, we shall continue to have mixed classes of boys and girls for all P.E. periods. If or when the time comes when this no longer seems desirable, we shall make different plans . . . It ought to be possible for there to be less compulsion for children who do not like outdoor games. Perhaps a games session in winter will include football, hockey or netball, dancing and some free choice. There should be no lack of playing fields

when we take over an extra 3½ acres of land formerly occupied by prefab houses.

The acquisition of the additional playing field space was an enormous asset, both from the physical education aspect and from an environmental point of view. Unfortunately, the optimism expressed over changing facilities never materialized. To this day, sensitive and discreet use of classrooms as changing areas has had to be the highly unsatisfactory answer.

A strange anomaly was created by the birth of the Middle School. Should it be classified as primary or secondary? At the special staff meeting the matter of school milk was raised, and Glover wrote in his notes:

> By law, senior children do not get an issue of free milk, and junior children do. It would appear that only the lower half of a middle school will receive the issue. However, a letter from the Divisional Education Office has laid down that the free issue of milk to middle school children will be discontinued.

On 22nd April 1970 there was a change of heart, which was recorded in the log:

> The supply of free milk to pupils of the lower school (former Junior age) was restored today after eighteen months without it. This was because the Ministry deemed a middle school to be secondary and secondary schools do not get free milk.

Shortly afterwards, any remaining muddle and confusion over the matter was eradicated by the permanent abolition of the daily third of a pint.

Northfield was one of the pioneers of the Middle School. Where the West Riding led, many other education authorities in Britain were to follow. Much of the log book from September 1968 to July 1969 was taken up with recording the laying down of firm Middle School foundations. In October the parents were briefed about all the implications of the change-over; County Council Inspector Selby made the first of many visits 'to check progress in a middle school;' and Northfield was visited by Mr Buxton, French adviser, 'who came to see how our French teaching was progressing.' During the course of the year, various members of Her Majesty's Inspectorate made appearances; students from Wentworth Castle, Barnsley, and Doncaster College of Education were shown around the school; the head of a Bradford school was the first in a long line of prospective middle school heads to visit Northfield; Ann Corbett, of the *New Society* magazine, included a visit to further her research for an article on new developments in education; and Michael Tucker (the prospective Conservative candidate for the parliamentary constituency of Hemsworth) called, presumably in the vain hope that by so doing he would boost his chances of overturning the largest Labour majority in the country at the next election.

Little else of import was recorded during that period. The first of many cultural visits to the Grand Theatre at Leeds was recorded when a party of staff and pupils watched a performance of *Swan Lake*, which was followed in due course by *The Sleeping Beauty* and *The Nutcracker* , and eventually a foray into the world of opera with *Carmen* and *La Traviata*. On 6th February 1969 the log recorded the opening ceremony, by Prince Philip, of Minsthorpe High School, to which the first Northfield pupils would soon be graduating.

Ominously, it was recorded on 13th November 1968 that 'The first really cold weather of the winter revealed again that the heating in our new hall is inadequate.' The following April, the purpose of one of C.C.I. Selby's visits was 'to discuss progress and problems of a Middle School, with particular attention to financial difficulties.'

Apart from that entry, there was no other hint of financial constraints until July 1969, when Glover decided to incorporate within the log a progress report on the first year of Northfield Middle School. He wrote: 'It has been decreed by the Ministry that a Middle School shall function and be classified as a Secondary School.' He stated that school milk was now abolished, to conform with Secondary principles, but 'we appear to be treated still as Primary Schools, particularly in respect of Allowances, Equipment, Capitation and Clerical Assistance.'

To promote music in school, the co-operation of parents was relied upon. There was no music room, and in order to maintain any music classes at all, Mrs Lindley had to employ a number of boys to push an already battered piano from room to room throughout the school. It was noted in the progress report that efforts were now being made to raise money to buy a portable electronic organ costing £140.

In his report the head expressed dismay that, with the first thirteen-year-olds ready to take their places, the promised heavy handicrafts room, containing woodwork and metalwork machinery, was still not ready. The conversion of a classroom for this purpose was still awaiting the removal of wooden floorboards and the installation of a concrete floor. Furthermore, the proposed domestic science room was awaiting completion.

His bitterness was further compounded by the state of affairs in physical education. The issue of the playing field was described as 'a most worrying time.' He continued, 'There are a number of Junior Football Leagues in the area, and our school governors believe that school facilities should be extended to such teams. As we have only one football pitch, it is deteriorating.' This was perfectly true, but as usual Glover was reluctant to extend Northfield facilities to all and sundry.

Ever the optimist, he concluded this part of his report with the following comment: 'It is still to be hoped to provide changing rooms, but no real progress has yet been made.'

In his report little space was devoted to academic achievement during the first year as a middle school. Only humanities was given specific mention:

> After one term we were not happy about some of the aspects of the work being done. A lack of urgency and a positive disinterest were observed amongst a number of children. Many were altogether too vague about what they were doing. We decided that too much freedom of choice had been given too quickly, and we reorganized this part of the teaching. We tried to mix some informal with formal and we have now hit on a reasonable blend. Children are now more positive about what they are doing and are enjoying the work.

The opportunity for bright, average and dull pupils to work together in humanities had distinct social advantages, but in due course the experiment proved to have too many disadvantages.

Some areas tended to be treated in greater depth than others, according to a teacher's individual strengths or weaknesses. I was strong in history; my colleague was a scientist, and geography received less attention than it deserved. Later I worked in harness with a skilled geography teacher but we both had self-confessed weaknesses in science, now that it was a more specialized subject than the old-fashioned junior school 'nature study'. Gradually it was accepted that the degree of specialization formerly expected in the secondary school could not be altogether denied in the upper years of a fully functioning middle school in subjects such as science. In time, humanities faded from the timetable and the individual subjects of history, geography and science assumed their rightful place.

Glover ended his report by reiterating his aims to establish team teaching and teaching units and to abolish streamed classes. No praise or criticism based on observations made over the past year was implied. It was as if he was merely reminding himself of the objectives he and his staff had set down for Northfield a year before, and convincing himself that they were still the right ones to pursue:

> We are trying to get children (and teachers) to think in terms of a year unit instead of the traditional class unit. We believe this is of fundamental importance, particularly to the less able sections of children. We find that to maintain the principle of non-streaming in a community with such a wide ability range requires a marked effort. We have to see that the influence of the natural leaders of any year of children has a chance to be felt by the others.

The log continued to assume a dull, characterless aspect, fulfilling the role of a systematic diary of visits and visitors and staff absences, spiced by the logging of the occasional accident to a pupil; for example:

> **9th October 1974**: Stanley Bucknall of the Third Year broke his collar bone whilst playing football. Taken with father to hospital by the headmaster.
>
> **23rd January 1975**: Julie Allott of the Fourth Year fainted in a

cookery class. Revival was very slow and incomplete and a doctor was sent for.

24th April 1975: Neil Makings, a Fourth Year Pupil, was knocked unconscious by a blow on the head from a cricket ball. He was taken home and then to hospital, where he was detained overnight.

17th November 1977: Pupil Paul Westwood required hospital treatment after a pencil had been prodded in his eye.

On one occasion an accident befell the teacher rather than the pupil:

20th January 1977: Mrs. J.A. Tulley hurt her neck whilst demonstrating backward roll in a P.E. lesson. Doctor diagnosed torn ligaments.

The entries in the log contrast strongly now with the lively comments which Glover used to put in before and during the days of reorganization. Williamson's log had been imposingly, impeccably written; it had been a matter of duty to write an almost daily detailed account of life in school and of such events in the community as might affect his school, and of course the log book had to be available at all times for inspection by governors, inspectors and other education officials. His entries were stamped with the dignity and authority of a highly respected leader. His was a hard act to follow. Swinbank did his best, but his entries could never match the aura created by the Williamson style. Then came Gordon, who built up such a huge reputation for the school and loved to extol that reputation wherever possible in his log. His sense of pride in the school was apparent with almost everything he wrote, and, unlike the other heads of Northfield, he could not resist allowing a dry sense of humour to creep into some of his comments. But now, in 1969, the character of the Northfield Log assumed an unprecedented ordinariness.

Now that the Middle School concept was fully operational, schools like Northfield became centres of national attention. The log records a constant stream of visitors from education authorities which were about to 'go middle', or were contemplating doing so. During 1969 and 1970 curious educationalists arrived from Normanton, Staffordshire, Leeds, Lincolnshire and Wiltshire. The following entry is typical:

> **26th February 1970**: Visited by Mr. Maurice Clark and Mr. B.B. Rowan of the Lincoln Diocesan Board of Education. They wished to see how an old school had been converted to a Middle School. They visited at the request of Sir Alec Clegg.

Pupils at Northfield became quite used to getting on with their work under the gaze of strangers, who seemed to speak in all sorts of peculiar dialects. For several years the stream of visitors continued, eventually subsiding to a trickle by the end of 1974, though in that year alone Mexborough, Newcastle-on-Tyne, Fife, Forfar, London, Gatwick and even Holland and Missouri U.S.A. were represented.

In order to meet with the West Riding Education Committee's wishes to promote still further the rôle of the Middle School within the comprehensive system, Jack Glover was asked to speak at a series of meetings. Such was his self-confidence and his love for expressing his views that he needed no persuading. At Sheffield University he spoke on 'Integrated work in a semi-open-plan school'; he addressed an audience at Keighley Teachers' Centre on 'The Middle School'; and at Crofton, 'The Headteacher and the Law' was the theme. On two occasions he was accompanied by members of his staff, for example:

> **6th June 1972**: Head, Deputy Head and two teachers gave a combined lecture on Middle School organisation at Leeds College of Education to an assembly of teachers attending a course.

Whenever possible, groups of pupils were taken out of school to pursue some aspect or other of the curriculum. In 1969-70, for instance, it was noted in the log that outings had taken place to Cusworth Hall, near Doncaster; to a Doncaster cinema to see *The Battle of Britain*; to Flamborough Head on a beach study; and to the premises of the *Doncaster Evening Post*, 'to see a newspaper being produced.' The most ambitious project that Northfield had ever undertaken, however, was a three-day educational visit to

London in December 1969. Typically, it was described in the log simply as 'A most successful venture'; no doubt Gordon or Williamson would have been far more effusive in similar circumstances. This outing was the first of several to London over the next few years. Though the log book is not expansive about them, they were the source of a store of memories for the staff and pupils involved: the thrill and excitement of high speed travel by British Railways and two nights spent in a comfortable Bayswater hotel; the delights of recognizing such landmarks as Buckingham Palace and the Houses of Parliament; visiting Regent's Park Zoo, the Tower of London, and Madame Tussaud's – and sailing down the Thames on a freezing December day; of Carole Roberts being sick all over the deputy head, Marjorie Maycock; of another member of staff, Andrew Cowling, being spat upon disgustingly by an angry llama (to the detriment of a very smart new suède jacket); and the shock and amazement felt by Mrs Lindley, the wife of the Vicar of South Kirkby, as the party walked through Soho on a Saturday evening.

Perhaps the supreme memory is of the misfortune which befell a pupil called Simon Woodward. It was customary on these excursions for all packing to be completed on the Sunday morning and the luggage dispatched to King's Cross Station, so that the party could enjoy an unencumbered walk through Regent's Park and round the Zoo before going for the train home in the afternoon. The walk through the park by the lakeside was carefree and leisurely, ducks were fed and photographs were taken. Whilst posing for a friend's camera, Simon was adjusting his position by walking slowly back a bit, back a bit, and – despite warnings from onlookers – he slid straight into Regent's Park Lake. Startled ducks fled noisily in all directions away from this unwelcome intruder, whilst members of staff hauled the lad, soaked to his chest, from the icy cold water. All the luggage was by now well on its way to King's Cross, so poor Simon had to endure a very uncomfortable couple of hours wearing an assortment of whatever dry garments other people could spare him.

Following the success of the London weekends, other ambitious projects were attempted, notably ones of an outward bound nature, to field centres and youth hostels. Such projects obviously required very careful, detailed preparation. Great emphasis was laid upon safety, and pupils were always left in no doubt about the correct equipment, footwear and clothing to take — or so it was thought. Ian, however, who had never been away from home except on day trips to Scarborough and Blackpool, turned up for a week's stay in Snowdonia, equipped for the mountains with nothing more suitable than a pair of black pumps. His friend Peter arrived at school ready for departure on the same outward bound course smartly dressed and carrying a brown suitcase. Completely ignorant of the nature of the venture, he had no sleeping bag or wet weather clothing.

The first foreign trip was a Fourth Year weekend in Paris, for which the relevant members of staff consulted an organization specializing in such educational ventures. It almost ended in disaster, when the hotel turned out to be a brothel! Hasty relocation was implemented and the weekend was completed successfully, to be followed in due course by a series of intricately planned and competently led winter sports breaks to Austria.

The Glover years came to an end when the fourth Headmaster of Northfield retired in July 1977. Glover's successor was Peter Nuttall, who attended the school as a pupil, returned as a student teacher and then after college became one of Glover's young protégés. He left in 1973 to be a deputy head in Woodlands, Doncaster — and now, in September 1977, returned yet again to take over the leadership of Northfield from his old mentor.

102   THE NORTHFIELD LOG

The Second Year, 1970-1971. Carol George made a special appearance (back row, 3rd from right). Also present here are Chris Westwood (4th row, 7th from left), and Simon Woodward (4th row, 6th from right).

13

Reminiscences

THIS CHAPTER is devoted to the reminiscences of a group of current Northfield teachers, whose experience there stretches back to the early days of the Glover era. They have recalled memories of more incidents and names which escaped the pages of the Northfield Log.

A Surfeit of Ice-Cream

Thirty years ago Sports Day was a far cry from the carefully organized, highly competitive event of today, with its fierce inter-house rivalry, record-keeping and a day-long programme of track and field events – the culmination of several weeks of training. In the old days a fine afternoon was chosen, more or less at random, and children were encouraged to participate in a series of flat races; for the less athletic there was a range of novelty races, such as the sack race and the potato race. The field was small, bumpy, and had an abundance of bare patches. The runners entered the events wearing more or less what they had come to school in that morning. Danny Oates's ice-cream van would call by and, to people like nine-year-old Kenneth, would be of infinitely more interest than events on the field. One of Kenneth's failings was that he was inclined to yield to temptation and over-indulge himself. He ate his fill of ice-cream and decided to save some for later.

The following morning he interrupted registration with the exclamation: 'Sir, sumbody's put ice-cream in me desk and it's melted all ovver me books!'

Stanley's Trifle

Before the Christmas Party succumbed to the charms of the disco, this event followed a rigid routine for many years. There were four parties, one for each year in school. They were held in the evening and as many members of staff as possible attended and assisted at each event. There was a set list of games and dances, such as The Grand Old Duke of York, Bobbing, Beetle, Musical Chairs, Pass the Parcel — and the climax was often a wild chasing game called Stir the Pudding, which owed its popularity to the opportunity for the children to 'whack' the teachers with a rolled-up newspaper. Just to make sure that everything went without a hitch, the programme was carefully rehearsed beforehand. All this activity was preceded by tea which, apart from the sandwiches, was provided by the parents. Boys and girls sat at tables of eight, each table laden with an assortment of food. Some parents could be relied upon to send in attractive iced buns, home-made cakes or pretty jellies or trifles. One could usually tell which child's parents were most likely to contribute the best items, and one would always hope to drop on a good table. The easiest option for parents, though, was a packet of biscuits or chocolate marshmallows and — no matter how fair the teachers tried to be when allocating the food to the tables — it always seemed that some tables were more insubstantially and unattractively served than others.

One year Stanley's mother promised to bake a rainbow cake for the party. He proudly handed the cake over to his teacher for slicing, at which point it was revealed that the bright layers of coloured sponge had all run together and the predominant colour of the rainbow was a dull grey. The following year Stanley's contribution was a huge glass dish of home-made trifle. The jelly was so runny that it had soaked up all of the sponge, fruit and blancmange; hundreds and thousands were dotted everywhere. The method of transporting it to school didn't help its condition much either. Because of its size, it was pushed to school in the bottom of an old pram.

Concert Catastrophe

For many years a regular feature of Northfield life has been its concerts, usually held at Christmas time or towards the end of the school year. The first took place in 1965 and consisted of some choral speaking, a gymnastics display and two or three comedy sketches, including a version of the nursery rhyme, 'Mary had a little lamb', all interspersed with items from the school choir. As the years went by, productions became more and more ambitious and the choir grew to such proportions that at times nearly half the school seemed to be in it. Perhaps the most spectacular and memorable of all Northfield productions was *Joseph and his Amazing Technicolour Dreamcoat*, which was staged in 1982.

Naturally, school productions are always subject to their little hitches. Children forget their lines at vital moments, faint in the choir or fall off the stage. One Christmas the shepherds were singing a solo, with the choir harmonizing softly in the background. All of a sudden there was an ear-shattering noise as of a prolonged burst of machine-gun fire. Miraculously, the soloists and choir carried on regardless. Their only problem was how, at the end of their performance, to vacate a stage now strewn with thousands of wooden beads, from a bead curtain which had been draped across the back of the stage and had chosen that particular moment to collapse.

Feinting Fit

It was morning registration in Bill Taylor's first year class. All was proceeding perfectly normally until a sudden hubbub arose around a girl, who had apparently fallen off her chair. 'Sir, it's Gail, I think she's fainted!' exclaimed the girl's neighbour, standing up in some alarm and stooping over the figure slumped on the floor.

'All right, sit down and clear out of the way!' snapped Taylor, striding across the classroom towards Gail. 'Open the door, somebody.'

As he bent down to pick up the limp form, he wondered how on earth she had managed to avoid bumping her head on the furniture. She looked a bit pale. His best plan would be to carry her to the staff room, alert the secretary and then make the patient comfortable . . . lay her down . . . blanket . . . water . . . cup of tea . . . His mind was racing ahead on such lines as he gently picked Gail up in his arms and headed towards the classroom door. Suddenly she opened her eyes, looked into his face, smiled angelically and said, 'April Fool, Sir!'

Pottery Class

A pottery session was in progress. A group of second years, under the guidance of their teacher, Miss Lappage, was modelling chickens. During the proceedings, two boys were quietly discussing where an egg comes from. Undecided, they asked their teacher, who gave them a simple explanation. At the end of the lesson, during the organized chaos of clearing up, Miss Lappage noticed that one of the models had an egg attached to the chicken's hind quarters and overheard one boy saying to the other: 'Ah'm nivver gunna eat another egg. They bloody shit 'em.'

Pig Swill

Jack Glover always took great pride in his appearance, tidily dressed in suit and tie, well groomed and shoes highly polished. He arrived at school one morning in December looking particularly smart, as he was to attend the school governors' special Christmas meeting in the afternoon.

Mr Fish kept pigs on a nearby allotment. He had a long-standing arrangement with the canteen staff to collect all the waste food for his pigs. It was stored in a dustbin which, with the help of a colleague, he would pick up once a week in his van. On this particular December morning the bin was unusually full – almost to the brim, in fact – and unfortunately Mr Fish was on his own. One of the canteen ladies volunteered her services, but the headmaster, who happened to be passing by at that moment, gallantly took over. The bin was lifted, carefully, and the two men proceeded cautiously, slowly, along a corridor towards the exit. There was a flight of five stone steps down to the yard. The van had been reversed as closely as possible to the steps, so that its floor was level with the third step. Now the well-tried technique was simple: drop the bin gently on the fourth step (whereupon the malodorous and nauseous mess plopped out over the brim and down Glover's suit and shoes and over the pig-man's overalls and boots), balance carefully, and then lower the bin gently on to the third step (with a repetition of the same disgusting effect), and now move the bin horizontally and slide it along the floor of the van.

Mr Fish expressed his gratitude and went on his way to see his pigs. The head was left ruing his spirit of gallantry and wondering how he was going to explain himself that afternoon.

A Special Case

There is a brief entry in the log on 9th September 1974 that 'Carol George, a former pupil at this school until she was sixteen years old (considered physically unfit to go to the High School), started duties as a Non-Teaching Assistant, but a special case.'

Carol's whole life was a battle against the odds. She was born with a congenital heart disease, for which the only cure would be the eventual replacement of a heart valve. As an infant, then through her childhood, she was very frail and extremely delicate; a permanent bluish tinge to her complexion was testament to her heart condition. School was out of the question, and she was educated at home until she was thirteen. At that age she was due to go to Minsthorpe High School, but such a step was considered so risky that, at a time when pupils normally left Northfield to go to Minsthorpe, arrangements were being made for Carol to have her first taste of real school life at Northfield. From 1971 to 1974 she was a member of the Fourth Year on a half-day basis. On her attaining the age of sixteen, her case was discussed at length at Wakefield, as full-time employment was considered impossible. As a result, a special post was created for her at Northfield on a mornings-only basis, in which Carol dealt with light secretarial duties.

In 1972, during her first year as a pupil at Northfield, she was considered old enough to undergo the first operation on her heart. This involved slicing into the main vein leading to the heart, the first time such a manœvre had been attempted. As a world's first, it merited a mention in the leading medical journals of the day. It was a success; sufficient pressure was relieved from her heart to enable Carol to cope adequately with her teenage years. However, it was understood that a further operation of major proportions would be essential on her reaching maturity if there was to be any chance of her leading a normal life thereafter.

For a while Carol showed improvement. Her complexion and her stamina both reflected a certain amount of optimism about her state of health. Her extremely sheltered life became a little more social. She had a steady boyfriend, Kevin Britton, an ex-Northfield pupil. An event took place which at one time was totally unimaginable − Carol and Kevin got married.

Carol was now in her twenties. Everyone knew that the time was drawing near for the big operation. Meanwhile, her most robust period of health seemed to be over. Her heart was showing obvious signs of struggling to cope with adulthood. Several times she was taken into hospital for tests and observation. All the time, she was gradually weakening, which did not augur well for the forthcoming operation.

She was 27 when, in 1985, she underwent the massive operation to replace the troublesome heart valve. Although she survived the operation, she was now in so weakened a condition that her brave struggle ended just a few days later.

Success

Teachers tend to lose track of the vast majority of the hundreds of children who pass through their hands. When pupils leave Northfield, they go through Minsthorpe and then enter the mainstream of life. Occasionally the news of the successes of past pupils filters into the staffroom and stirs memories. Reports of academic achievement, such as a degree in law or astrophysics, bring especial pleasure. A few ex-Northfield students have made a career in teaching; one notable example is remembered as a frail, puny child whose health problems suggested that any sort of career would be virtually unthinkable; ultimately, her indomitable spirit overcame all.

Ex-Northfield lads have successfully joined the ranks of the armed forces and the police. Others have gone into professional sport, playing locally for Frickley Athletic and making appearances further afield for league football teams. One well-remembered lad is in his element as a gamekeeper, another as a garage proprietor. An ex-Northfield girl is now chief personnel officer for a metropolitan borough; another has achieved success in a male-dominated world as a qualified civil engineering technician, with special responsibility for highways and sewage; another girl is remembered as having difficult times at Northfield but has found success and family security in Australia.

I get a strange sense of pride when I discover that the person pulling my pint in a pub is a former pupil of mine; that the smartly dressed young man showing me to my restaurant table used to go to Northfield; that the lady bus driver accepting my fare was in my class not so many years ago; or that the young cashier at the bank learnt some of her maths in my classroom. I was particularly pleased some years ago when I took a party of children from Northfield to Conisbrough Castle, to be greeted unexpectedly and conducted around the grounds by the curator, another former pupil of mine. Even in hospital there is no escaping the influence of Northfield. On a recent stay in Pontefract General Infirmary, two of the nurses who ministered to me were ex-pupils – while a third, I learned later, was on duty in the operating theatre.

Whilst most achieve varying degrees of success, very few achieve fame. One former student of Northfield, however, is on the threshold of that rare distinction. Chris Westwood attended there from 1969 to 1973. At the age of ten he already displayed enormous powers of imagery and revealed a depth of vocabulary far beyond what would be expected of the average middle school pupil. A memorable pastiche of the 'Dracula' story showed an early leaning towards science fiction and horror.

In its infancy, Minsthorpe failed to do justice to his rare talents. On leaving there, he went into pop music journalism, working for *Record Mirror* from 1978 until 1981. Careerwise, this did not seem to be very fulfilling, so he made a break into film and television production, embarking on a two-year course at Bournemouth Film School. From there he decided to risk all in full-time

110   THE NORTHFIELD LOG

writing. His first published novel, *A Light in the Black*, appeared in 1989, followed by *Personal Effects* and *Calling all Monsters*, aimed chiefly at the teenage market. Judging by the public reaction to these early works, however, it will not be long before his horizons become illimitable, as his work has already been likened to that of Stephen King and has begun to attract the attention of Steven Spielberg. Could it be that Northfield has helped to spawn an international literary talent?

The First Year, 1988

14

A Community Undermined

IF ANYTHING, Peter Nuttall's ordeal as Head of Northfield has been even more challenging than Jack Glover's in that office. He was fortunate in inheriting a settled and successful middle school, but gradually an insidious unease was creeping into the environment. South Kirkby was feeling the first rumblings of unrest, which were to lead to the steady decline and fall of a mining community.

When unrest in the mining industry finally erupted into the year-long Miners' Strike of 1984-1985, the pupils of Northfield could hardly be expected to carry on as if nothing was happening. Fathers and elder brothers were out on strike and involved in the bitter picketing conflicts; little money was coming into the homes; mothers were struggling to make ends meet. The philosophy of the school continued to be one based on the upholding of the law of the land and belief in the strength and wisdom of British justice; but that philosophy was sorely tested now. Children were well aware of the violence resulting from some of the picketing, of the pilfering of coal from the pit yards and tips, and of the vandalizing of trees and fences for firewood. Whilst having every sympathy with the plight of local families, the school still had to maintain its rôle of educator and upholder of correct behaviour.

Great care had to be taken at all times in school to show no prejudice or favour to either side in the conflict. The school was used as a station for the distribution of free lunches to miners' children, and full and discreet co-operation was given in this respect. Despite the use of as much tact and discretion as the Northfield staff could muster, angry — but baseless — rumours spread through the district, claiming that the headmaster had allowed police into school to question children of striking miners about incidents of illegal picketing. An incensed and offended Nuttall had to request the intervention of the local branch of the National Union of Mineworkers to calm matters. Such an incident as this was typical of those uneasy times. Even today, a decade later, pockets of animosity and resentment towards the police emerge from time to time. It has been no easy task to restore children's faith and confidence in their local policemen.

The mining community was very close-knit; it had immense pride in its ability to dig out a dirty and dangerous living deep underground. Now, the local mining community is no more. The 1980s saw it fight, struggle spiritedly, then disintegrate and finally disappear. The pits dominated the local industrial scene for a hundred years. Shops and services are now in a state of decline; job opportunities are scarce; petty crime is on the increase. The gradual fragmentation of a traditionally close-knit community in South Kirkby has been accompanied by a widespread undermining of family values. The onus of the teacher becomes more than ever one of social worker as well as educator.

1988 brought along the National Curriculum, the institution of which has drastically changed the rôle of every head and every teacher in the land. Strict requirements are now laid down to govern the ways of teaching every subject in every year. More time than ever before must be devoted to the upkeep of progress records for every pupil in every subject on the curriculum. Testing in the core subjects is to be carried out at the ages of 7, 11 and 14. At first sight the teacher appears to have been deprived of the freedom to teach a subject with his own individual flair or style. At first sight the week's timetable would appear to need elasticated sides in order to accommodate all the requirements of the National Curriculum. Perhaps, in time, bearing in mind the good teacher's skills in adaptation and versatility and the National Curriculum Council's own plans for modification, a satisfactory compromise will be reached.

Nuttall's log contains scarcely any reference to the Miners' Strike of 1984-1985, or to the inception of the National Curriculum. Although it is still regarded as an official document, the log is now virtually obsolete. It is still very occasionally used as a

A COMMUNITY UNDERMINED

diary, but it is seldom asked for. Now, indeed, it rarely sees the light of day.

Most other aspects of record-keeping in school have become computerized, with information kept on disk. Northfield has its own computer system linked directly with the Education Office in Wakefield. If the Northfield Log is to survive, maybe it too will be refined into a disembodied micro-chip, while the beautiful dip-and-scratch copperplate of former years will be but a distant memory.

Peter Nuttall's anxiety-ridden time continues. His current worry is one which is shared, no doubt, by everyone who has, for one reason or another, developed an affinity with his school – in the proposed shake-up of local education in 1996, what is to become of Northfield?

The Northfield Staff, 1988

114 THE NORTHFIELD LOG

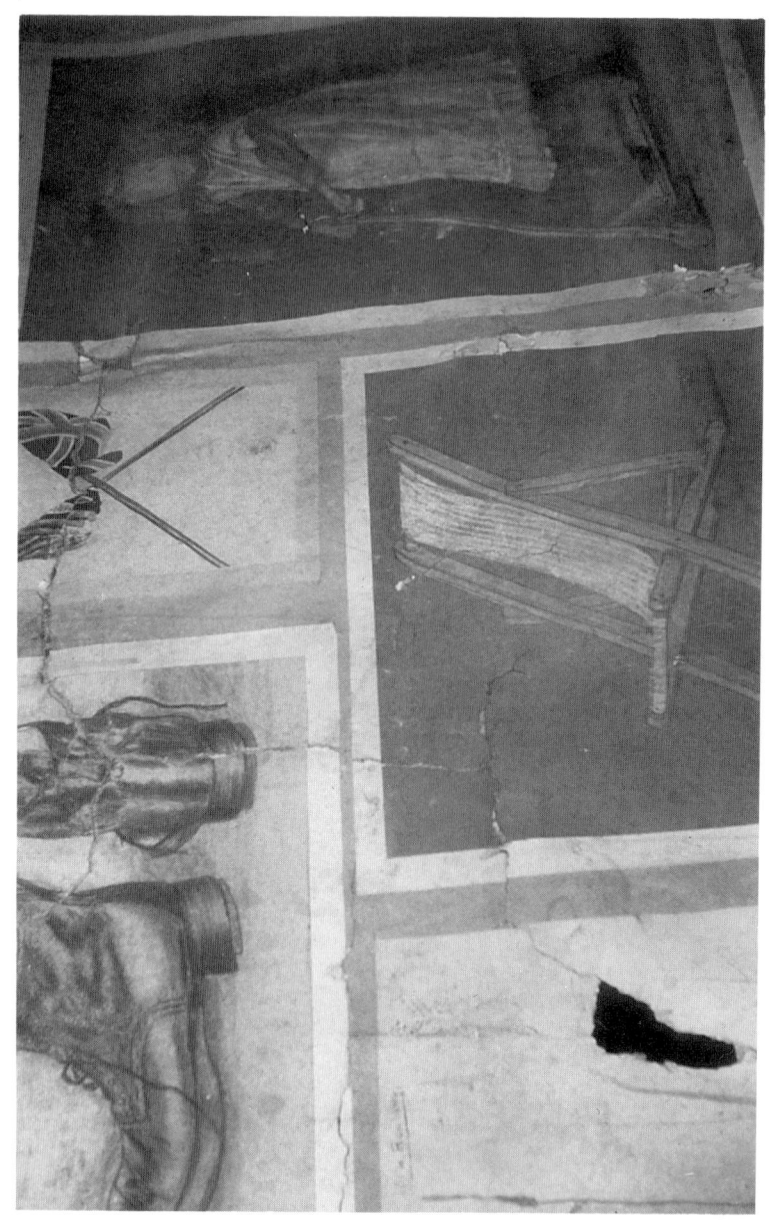

Link with the past. Part of art display produced at Northfield in 1917 and still on show there today.

15

The Future of Northfield

PLANS FOR REORGANIZATION were mooted in a series of Southern Area Review documents published by the Wakefield Education Committee in the early 1980s. These were based on changeover from first to middle school at 8, and to high school at 12. Eventually the scheme was shelved; perhaps this was just as well, as the introduction of the National Curriculum in 1988, advocating testing at 7, 11 and 14, would have meant a very early re-think.

In October 1991 the Chief Education Officer contacted heads in the Hemsworth and Minsthorpe pyramids, stating that, in view of the National Curriculum's key stage assessments at the ages of 7, 11 and 14, attention was again being focused on what would be the most appropriate ages of transfer. A major consultation exercise was already under way in Wakefield City, Crigglestone and Woolley, and in the Castleford and Airedale pyramids, with a view to proposed changes. Heads' comments were invited.

By the end of that year the heads had reported back. They were virtually unanimous in their agreement that the time was right for a change in the ages of transfer. A report from the Chief Education Officer dated 24th March 1992 stated: 'The implications of the National Curriculum, and the increasing difficulty of recruiting specialist teaching staff into the 9-13 middle schools, led headteachers to that view.' The same report continued: 'Many heads are reluctant to see the abolition of the middle school system. The Hemsworth and Minsthorpe areas were pioneers in the late 1960s, where first, middle and high schools were first introduced, and they have served the pupils of the area well over the last 25 years. Heads are rightly proud of their achievements.'

The next stage was the publication, in March 1992, of a consultation document entitled 'Schools for Tomorrow'. More reasons were put forward as to why a review was considered necessary:

> To enable schools to plan their development effectively;
>
> To respond to changing patterns of school population;
>
> To use limited resources as effectively as possible;
>
> To meet the targets considered by the Department of Education and Science when it decides the Local Education Authority's allocation for capital spending;
>
> To improve the quality of school accommodation in the Southern Area.

It was pointed out that the Hemsworth and Minsthorpe schools were currently supporting too many surplus places. An estimated £477,000 per year was being spent on maintaining unneeded places in that area. If, say, a target of about 900 surplus places were removed in the process of reorganization, resulting in the possible closure of some schools, the money saved would form a significant contribution towards the cost of the substantial building improvements that would be necessary. 'The L.E.A. is most unlikely to be allocated the finance to do the work unless it can be shown that the project is economical according to D.E.S. criteria.' Once again, local interested parties were invited to discuss ways forward and report back to County Hall.

By October 1992 another big response had been generated from teachers, parents, governors and interested members of the public, reiterating their general agreement with changeover at 7 and 11, and expressing optimism about the creation of Junior Mixed and Infants' schools, with nursery facilities wherever possible. There was a feeling of unease, however, about the potentially overwhelming size of the high schools that admission at eleven would create. A popular suggestion was the provision of a third high school, located possibly at Felkirk or Ackworth. The Chief Education Officer undertook to consider the feasibility of such a scheme. He also declared that capital expenditure of around £13 to £15 million would be necessary to carry out reorganization. At a meeting of the Education Committee, on 13th

October 1992, it was resolved that plans should now be prepared for reorganization based on transfer to high school at age eleven, and that those plans should provide for the retention of sixth forms at Hemsworth and Minsthorpe.

At long last the projected future of Northfield was discussed in another consultation document, released on 2nd February 1993. It was proposed that South Kirkby should have three J.M.I. schools for pupils of age 5-11 – two sharing a catchment area south of the main road, namely Burntwood and Stockingate, and Northfield serving all of the town to the north of the main road. Common Road, currently housing a middle and a first school, would close. 'The Education Authority would seek to provide a new school building at Northfield to replace the existing sub-standard premises.'

Could the powers that be afford to meet the enormous financial outlay that a new Northfield would demand? Or would they settle for the only slightly less enormous outlay which would be required to put the battered old building into the Twentieth Century, let alone fit it for the new millenium?

The Education Committee's proposals brought forth an interesting counter-proposal from a host of aggrieved Common Road supporters: keep Common Road and Northfield open as two large J.M.I.s serving opposite ends of South Kirkby, and close down the two newer schools, Burntwood and Stockingate.

The prospective size of the high schools continued to cause concern. Minsthorpe, at a possible 1600 pupils, was not quite so worrying as Hemsworth, at 1950, but a suggestion to alleviate the latter's problem somewhat by ceding Ryhill and Havercroft to the Crofton High School catchment area was of interest to the Committee. An unnamed correspondent wrote to County Hall with another interesting suggestion: the size of both Minsthorpe and Hemsworth could be reduced by building a new school on the old colliery site midway between South Kirkby and Hemsworth. There seems to be no further mention of this idea.

The Chief Education Officer published the recommendations of the Education Committee in July 1993, having studied the reactions to the document issued earlier that year. There was a slight change of heart, in that Stockingate was now to become a junior school and Common Road First was to remain open as that area's infant department and nursery. Common Road Middle was to close. That was final. Burntwood and Northfield were to become junior and infant schools, both with nursery departments. Northfield would have about 245 on roll, plus a nursery allocation of 26.

'At Northfield,' it was stated, 'a major capital investment will be essential. Most of the premises are now 90 years old, though the main hall dates from 1968. The building will need major rehabilitation.'

No further commitment is made at this stage as to whether the old building is to be modernized or whether a completely new building is planned. It appears to be simply a question of what the D.E.S. will sanction. It is stated, in the report of July 1993, that 'The capital costs of the proposals . . . are expected to come to £15 – £20 million.'

The Education Committee gave its final consent to the reorganization proposals on 14th September 1993. They were then submitted to the Department of Education and Science. The Secretary of State announced his approval of the Minsthorpe area plans in the summer of 1994.

As for Northfield, it was finally decided, after many inspections, much letter writing and frequent discussions, that the fabric of the original building was still sound and good for another hundred years. No new school building would be needed on the site.

In July 1995 the Head of Northfield, Peter Nuttall, brought the school's story right up to date with the following remarks:

'The implementation of plans drawn up to convert Northfield Middle School into Northfield Junior and Infants with Nursery is scheduled to commence in November 1995. Renovation work, expected to cost in the region of half a million pounds, should be completed by December 1996. All of the structural alterations will be internal. Walls erected during the conversions to Middle School status are to be removed as part of the process of creating a new staff-room, a music room and nursery facilities. The heating system is to be upgraded, certain areas are to have new floors, and new toilet facilities are to be installed' — though those long-vaunted plans for showers and changing rooms seem destined to remain for ever on the drawing board — 'so Northfield's final year as a Middle School promises to be an interesting one.'

THE FUTURE OF NORTHFIELD

'Changes in personnel are inevitable. Many long-established members of the staff have indicated that they may take the opportunity offered by reorganization to seek early retirement. Among them will be the Head, Peter Nuttall. His successor will be Martin Dove, the present Head of the soon-to-be-redundant Common Road Middle School.

'Much remains to be done during the last few months before the changeover; teaching, clerical and caretaking staff to be appointed; the new school's organization, ethos and philosophy to be thought through and developed — a daunting and difficult task. The prospect which lies ahead is an exciting one, as Northfield prepares to enter a new millenium and approaches its own centenary. Good luck, Northfield! May you continue to thrive as the proud educator of the children of South Kirkby for another hundred years.'

APPENDIX A

**Four Hundred Years
of
Educational Opinion**

*And then the whining schoolboy, with his satchel,
And shining morning face, creeping like snail
Unwillingly to school.*
>William Shakespeare (1564-1616)
>*As You Like It*

*Skill comes so slow, and life so fast doth fly,
We learn so little and forget so much.*
>Sir John Davies (1569-1626)

We live and learn, but not the wiser grow.
>John Pomfret (1667-1703)
>*Reason*

A little learning is a dangerous thing.
>Alexander Pope (1688-1744)
>*Essay on Criticism*

It is no matter what you teach them first, any more than what leg you shall put into your breeches first.
>Samuel Johnson (1709-1784)

There is now less flogging in our great schools than formerly, but then less is learned there; so that what the boys get at one end they lose at the other.
>Samuel Johnson (1709-1784)

Let schoolmasters puzzle their brain,
With grammar, and nonsense, and learning.
Good liquor, I stoutly maintain,
Gives genius a better discerning.
>Oliver Goldsmith (1728-1774)
>*She Stoops to Conquer*

Example is the school of mankind, and they will learn at no other.
>Edmund Burke (1729-1797)

Come forth into the light of things,
Let Nature be your teacher.
>William Wordsworth (1770-1850)
>*The Tables Turned*

I don't know . . . why they make all this fuss about education.
>Viscount Melbourne (1779-1848)

He never spoils the child and spares the rod,
But spoils the rod and never spoils the child.
>Thomas Hood (1799-1845)
>*The Irish Schoolmaster*

The years teach much, which the days never know.
>Ralph Waldo Emerson (1803-1882)

Upon the education of the people of this country the fate of this country depends.
>Benjamin Disraeli (1804-1881), speaking in the House of Commons in 1874

To make your children capable of honesty is the beginning of education.
>John Ruskin (1819-1900)

Education has for its object the formation of character.
> Herbert Spencer (1820-1903)
> *Social Statics*

Soap and education are not as sudden as a massacre, but they are more deadly in the long run.
> Mark Twain (1835-1910)

He who can, does. He who cannot, teaches.
> George Bernard Shaw (1856-1950)
> *Maxims for Revolutionists*

Teach us delight in simple things,
And mirth that has no bitter springs;
Forgiveness free of evil done,
And love to all men 'neath the sun!
> Rudyard Kipling (1865-1936)
> *The Children's Song*

Human History becomes more and more a race between education and catastrophe.
> H.G. Wells (1866-1946)
> *The Outline of History*

Child! do not throw this book about;
Refrain from the unholy pleasure
Of cutting all the pages out!
Preserve it as your chiefest treasure.

... Your little hands were made to take
The better things and leave the worse ones:
They also may be used to shake
The massive paws of elder persons.
> Hilaire Belloc (1870-1953)
> *Bad Child's Book of Beasts*

APPENDIX B

SIR ALEC CLEGG

The West Riding's last Chief Education Officer

September 1996 marks the end of an era in which Northfield played a prominent and pioneering role. When it first became a middle school, in September 1968, it was acting very much as a guinea pig. But where Northfield (one of a small, select band of schools) was to lead, albeit warily at first, with the nation's spotlight glaring upon it, many others were soon to follow. In January 1968 there were no middle schools anywhere in Britain. In 1978 there were almost 1700.

The launching of the Middle School, and its consequent success, can be attributed to a large extent to the perspicacity and perseverance of Sir Alec Clegg, who was Chief Education Officer for the West Riding of Yorkshire from 1942 until 1974.

Alexander Bradshaw Clegg was born in 1909 and educated at Long Eaton County Secondary School in Nottinghamshire, where his father was headmaster. He continued his education at Bootham School, York, before going on to read modern languages at Clare College, Cambridge. Subsequently he took an M.A. degree after part-time studies at King's College. He became the Chief Education Officer for the West Riding at the unusually early age of 33 and was the last person to hold that post, his retirement in 1974 coinciding with the abolition of the West Riding County Council.

He pioneered many ideas in education, the most notable of which led to a new three-tier system in schools and the birth of the Middle School. At his instigation the education authority acquired such properties as Ingleborough Hall, Grantley Hall, Woolley Hall (now an in-service teachers' centre) and Bretton Hall (a teachers' training college whose grounds accommodate the prestigious Yorkshire Sculpture Park).

He received a knighthood for his services to education in 1965, the year in which he served as president of the Chief Education Officers' Association. Other awards included honorary fellowships of Bretton Hall College of Higher Education and King's College, London; honorary degrees from the universities of Leeds, Loughborough and Bradford; and the Étoile Noire from the French government. He was a member of United Nations Educational, Scientific and Cultural Organization delegations to Uruguay and the Philippines. Yet he still found time to write books on education, such as *About Our Schools* and, with his wife, to take an active part in church life in their home village of Saxton, near Tadcaster.

Until 1964 transfer to secondary school was fixed by law at the age of eleven. Local authorities had to provide 25% of grammar school places free, those places being allocated through a competition known as the 'Eleven Plus'. The age of eleven was deemed to be the age at which adolescence commenced. The 1944 Education Act had made a very clear distinction between primary and secondary pupils, with a virtually unbridgeable gulf at that peculiar age of eleven. Such a proposal as that which Sir Alec Clegg put forward in 1963 was bound to have to struggle for recognition. After all, to contemplate a reorganization on three-tier lines – five to nine, nine to thirteen and thirteen plus – was not only to contravene a long-held educational belief, but also to contravene the law.

Other comprehensive schemes were already afoot elsewhere in the country. However, as it was laid down that the age of transfer must be eleven, considerable overcrowding was now being felt in the new comprehensive high schools, whose function was to combine the old secondary modern with the traditional grammar schools. That age-span, from eleven to eighteen, was becoming unmanageable in Sir Alec's view. For a number of reasons, transition at thirteen was much more viable. With the abolition of the 'Eleven Plus' for selection to the traditional grammar school, educational inequality would be eradicated; middle schools would provide a nice balance between primary and secondary principles; middle schools would be able to extend the primary schools' potential for assisting pupils during a critical stage in their personal development; specialization need not be a factor with the twelve and thirteen year olds, except in French; and the pressure exerted on oversized high schools would be alleviated.

Furthermore, if the school leaving age were to be raised to sixteen, the high schools would still have three years to prepare their pupils for 'O' levels and C.S.E.'s, so that children up to thirteen would no longer be subject to examination traumas.

Matters now began to move apace. Sir Edward Boyle's Education Act of 1964 gave a boost to Sir Alec's initiative by legalizing a change in the age of transfer. Permission was also granted for the building of new middle schools; but the Act made it clear that middle schools were to be regarded as part primary and part secondary, with greater financial advantages to the latter. (In fact, after its inception the middle school remained an anomalous, almost ephemeral creation; it certainly existed, but as all education had to be termed primary, secondary or further, 'middle' was never officially acknowledged.)

The new Labour government of 1964 declared itself committed to the reorganization of secondary education on non-selective lines. The Central Advisory Council for Education, through the Plowden Report of 1967, recommended middle schools which would combine traditional work with the best of primary education. The Report expressed a preference for an eight-twelve age range, but there was no need for Sir Alec to revise his nine-thirteen plans for the West Riding, as a further recommendation was to lead to the raising of the school leaving age to sixteen, thus ensuring that pupils in the new high schools would be guaranteed three years to prepare for major examinations.

By the time the Plowden Report was published, the first middle schools in the country were close to becoming a reality. Then came that momentous day when, after 2½ years of what Jack Glover described as 'unspeakable disorder and inconvenience', Northfield opened its doors as a middle school on 9th September 1968.

It was one of the first of its kind, yet it was created somewhat inadequately and at small expense out of an old, cold and ill-equipped building. It deserved better than to be a new educational format in antiquated surroundings; it was just another example of the financial pressure squeezed on certain authorities by the government. This lack of resources had long been one of Sir Alec's chief bones of contention.

On 8th January 1974, just before his retirement, he said (as reported in an article in the *Yorkshire Post*): 'One of the West Riding's main problems has always been the lack of money. In 1945 total expenditure per year was £4,700,000, and even though it has risen over the last thirty years, . . . it is still the poorest in the country.' He complained that 'Government distribution of money . . . to local authorities has consistently favoured the richer areas. Places like Kent, Sussex and Hertfordshire, all areas with a significantly higher average standard of living than the West Riding, seem to get a bigger slice of the financial cake. . . . We know now the extent to which disadvantage affects a child's performance at school, and this disadvantage is concentrated in this part of the world. Yet the finance is not distributed according to need.' He described how, despite severe financial constraints, the West Riding forged on and set national standards in the field of in-service training, in the promotion of the arts in schools and in the support given to the under-achiever.

Sir Alec expressed particular pride in the latter cause: 'In 1945 junior school education was centred on the basis of the "Three R's" and preparation for the "Eleven Plus". A child was either dim, bright or middling.' Over the next thirty years Sir Alec and the West Riding set out to show that this was a totally unfair and simplistic method of estimating a child's ability and that no child should be 'written off as a dud' at an early age. 'Pioneering schools like South Kirkby Junior' – Northfield – 'and Rossington Junior started to demonstrate that just because a youngster spoke with a heavy Yorkshire accent, came from a poor home and was not much good at English or maths, it did not necessarily mean he was a no-hoper at everything. For the first time we were beginning to see what the children of average and below average ability could really achieve – it was a revolution in the primary school.'

Equality was extremely important to Sir Alec. He had a natural sympathy for the underdog, who after all trod the same earth and breathed the same air as his more academically gifted fellows. What he did in the pursuit of equal opportunity in the primary field, he proceeded to achieve on a larger scale still by fighting for the establishment of the Middle School. In *Middle Schools: Ori-*

gins, Ideology and Practice, edited by Hargreaves and Tickle, middle schools are described as having been 'hurled into existence by the innovatory and proselytizing zeal of various educational reformers such as Sir Alec Clegg, who might be seen to have conducted an educational crusade in the pursuit of openness and change.'

More change is imminent with the demise of the Middle School, but nothing will change the memory of Sir Alec Clegg as a great educational crusader.

Sir Alec Clegg

Index

accidents, 57, 61, 62, 79-80, 97-98, 100
Acts of Parliament:
   Balfour (1902), 1
   Coal Mines (1912), 35
   Education (1944), 80
   Education (1964), 125
   Forster (1870), 2
   Mundella (1880), 3
   Provision of Meals (1906), 34, 46, 80
'Aeroplane Week' (1918), 42
air raids, 41, 66, 70
air raid shelters, 66, 69
April Fools Day, 105-6
Armistice (1918), 42, 44
Ascension Day, 65-6
Asquith, Herbert, 34-5
Attenborough, 'Dickie,' (Lord Attenborough), vii-ix, 77
attendance at school, 9-11, 15-16, 18, 27, 41, 51, 55, 57, 65

Baldwin, Stanley, 47
Battersea Training College, 5
Belgian Relief Fund, 38-9
Bell, Andrew, 1, 2
'Bi-lateral Grouping', 92-3
Board School, 1, 2, 3, 5, 10, 15, 17
Boys' Brigade, 88
Broad Lane School, South Elmsall, 30
Burntwood First School, 83, 117, 118

Cambrai (Battle of, 1917), 41-2
Chelsea Training College, 5, 6
Christmas in School, 26, 29-30, 104-5
'Church School', 2, 3, 4, 8, 18, 42
'Circular on Ventilation', 23
circus (menagerie), 10, 55, 57
clay work, 77-8, 106
Clegg, Sir Alec, vii-viii, 76, 77, 99, 123-7
clothing, 8, 33, 51, 52, 65

Common Road Schools, 117, 118
Comprehensive Education, 83, 92, 123-5
concerts, 29, 30, 105
Cook, Arthur (Sec., M.F.G.B.), 50
Coronation (1911), 29-30
corporal punishment, 53, 54, 64
Crofton High School, 117
curriculum:
   art, 12-13, 42, 65, 75-8, 93, 114
   domestic science, 62, 96
   drawing, 12-13
   'drill', 26
   English, 11-12, 76, 92, 93
   environmental studies, 72-3
   French, 92, 94-5
   geography, 25, 27, 76, 92, 97
   handicraft, 27, 62, 96, 106
   history, 25, 76, 92, 97
   'housewifery', 27
   'humanities', 92, 96
   maths (arithmetic), 11, 25, 92
   music, 93, 95-6
   'nature study', 27, 76, 97
   physical education / games, 26, 58, 59, 61, 64, 74, 84, 93-4, 96
   poetry, 12
   Religious Instruction, 93
   science, 62, 92, 97

dancing, 63
Dartington Hall, Devon, 77
Dickinson, Mary (pupil-teacher), 7
'Dig for Victory', 70
disease, 8, 20-21, 42-3, 55, 58, 61, 63, 65
Doncaster Races, 55, 60

'Education Week' (1924), 59
'Eleven Plus', 83, 92, 124, 126
'Empire Day', 60
epidemics, 20-21, 42-3, 65

INDEX

evacuation, 70-71

fire drill, 59, 61, 62
First World War (The Great War), 38-44, 45
Fish, Mr (The Pig Man), 106-7
Fletcher, J.S., 3-4
food, emergency provision of, 34-5, 46, 50, 52, 66
Frickley Colliery, 4, 35
Frickley Colliery Band, 59

Gannon, Tom, 91
general elections, 29, 30, 59
General Strike (1926), 50
George, Carol, 102, 107-8
Gotha (war-plane), 41
Green Lane School, Bradford, 80

H-, Harry & Kate (parents), 61
Harper, Ada (pupil-teacher), 23
health and hygiene, 6, 8, 9, 20-21, 42-3, 52, 58-9, 62, 63, 78-9, 81
heating, 21-24, 51, 75, 78, 79, 83-4
Hemsworth Grammar School, 65-83
Hemsworth High School, 83, 116, 117
Hinchcliffe, Sir James, 52
Hirst, Isabella (monitress), 7
H.M.I. (His Majesty's Inspectors) Reports:
  1903: 9, 13, 14-16
  1922: 48-49
  1930: 61-62
  1935: 65
  1950: 75,78
holidays, 10, 11, 20, 29, 37, 43, 56-7, 70
Hutt, Thomas, 2

'Integrated Teaching', 93

Kay-Shuttleworth, Sir James, 5

Lancaster, Joseph, 1, 2

magic lantern, 26-7
malnutrition, 34-5, 45, 46, 50, 52, 66
May Day, 71, 85
meals in school, 34, 46, 80-83
Miller, Maud Reeta (pupil-teacher, 7
Miners' Association of Great Britain, 45
Miners' Battalion, 39, 41
Miners' Federation of Great Britain, 33, 35, 45, 46
Miners' Gala, 10, 29

Miners' Relief Fund (1926), 51
Miners' Strike (1912), 33-7, 80
Miners' Strike (1921), 45-7
Miners' Strike (1926), 35, 50-52
Miners' Strike (1984-1985), 111-112
Minimum Wage Principle, 33
Minsthorpe High School, 83, 95, 108, 109, 115, 116, 117
Monitorial System, 1, 2, 7
Moorthorpe School, 56, 80

National Curriculum, 112, 115
National School, xiv, 2, 3, 4, 5
National Society, 1, 2
National Union of Mineworkers, 112
National Union of Railwaymen, 55
Naturalist Trust, 75
New Society magazine, 95
Northfield Heads:
  Glover, J.T., 82, 84, 86, 87-9, 91-101, 106-7
  Gordon, D., 72-82, 87, 98
  Nuttall, P., xi-xii, 86, 101, 111-113
  Swinbank, J., 63, 69, 71, 72, 98
  Williamson, F., 5-9, 13, 17-24, 25-30, 34, 35, 39, 40, 41, 44, 50, 62, 98
Northfield Lane Council School, 65, 67, 68
Northfield Lane Junior Mixed School, 84, 89
Northfield Methodist Chapel, xiv, 5, 6, 82
Northfield Middle School, 83, 84, 91-101
Northfield Pupils:
  Allott, Julie, 97-8
  Britton, Kevin, 108
  Bucknall, Stanley, 97
  Gail, 105-6
  George, Carol, 102, 107-8
  Ian, 101
  Kenneth, 103
  Makings, Neil, 98
  Peter, 101
  Rhodes, Arthur, 27
  Roberts, Carol, 100
  Stanley, 104
  Westwood, Chris, 102, 108-110
  Westwood, Paul, 98
  Woodward, Simon, 100, 102
Northfield Teachers:
  Atkins, Marjorie, 70
  Chapman, Charles, 40, 43, 56, 57, 61, 62
  Cowling, Andrew, 100
  Crossley, Mrs Clara, 6, 7, 17, 19
  Davies, Miss Mary, 6, 7

Lappage, Miss Mary, 106
Lindley, Mrs C., 95-6, 100
Maycock, Miss Marjorie, 100
R-, Mr A., 63-5
Sharpe, Mrs Emily, 19, 20, 40, 56, 57
Street, Arthur, 39-40
Taylor, William, 105-6
Thistlethwaite, Miss Phyllis, 40
Thorpe, Joseph, 70, 75
Todd, Mark, 40, 43
Tulley, Mrs Jean, 98
Widdowson, Miss, 40, 43
Northumberland Fusiliers, 40
Nottingham, Mrs Elizabeth, 2

outings (day), 27-8, 57, 58, 60, 72-3, 75, 99
outings (cultural), 60, 65, 75, 95
outings (longer):
London, 100
Paris, 101
Snowdonia, 101
Staithes Camp, 61
winter sports, 101
overcrowding, 7, 8, 18, 19, 78, 79, 80, 82

Parkin, Mary Ann, 2
Pearson, 'Skipper', 75
'pink-eye, 21
Plowden Report (1967), 125
poverty, 33-5, 45-52
pupil-teachers, 5, 7, 23

Remembrance Day, 60
Royal Fleet Auxiliary, 40
Royal Funeral (1936), 65
Royal Tank Corps, 42
Royal Visit (Minsthorpe, 1969), 95
Royal Weddings (1922, 1923), 57
Rural Education Exhibition (1912), 29

salaries, 56
'Salute the Soldier Week' (1944), 71
Schilling, Mr, 2, 4
School Board, 2, 9, 10, 15-16
School Meals Service, 80-82, 82-3
school milk, 94, 95

school reports, 67-8
'Shopping Week' (1928), 60-61
Soup Kitchen, 46
'Southern Area Review,' 115-117
South Kirkby Agricultural Show (1914), 29, 38
South Kirkby Colliery, 3, 4, 33-5, 111-112
South Kirkby Wesleyan Sunday School, 5-16, 118
Southmoor Road School, Hemsworth, 30
'Spanish 'Flu' ('Spanish Lady'), 43
Sports Day, 43, 56, 58, 60, 103
staffing, 5, 7, 18-19, 39, 40, 43
'Standards', 11, 12, 17, 18, 19
Stockingate School, 117
Sunday School Treats, 10, 18
swimming baths, 74
syllabus, 11-12, 92-3, 97

Temperance Movement, 27, 58
Thompson, Robert (of Kilburn), 73
toilets, 9, 13, 14, 15, 17, 60, 78-9, 83, 84
'Tradesmen's Concert', 29
Trades Union Congress, 47, 50
training colleges, 5, 7
truancy, 9-10

V.E. Day, 71
ventilation, 23-4
Village Circulating Library, 59
visitors, 76-78, 94-5, 98-9

Wakefield Education Authority (West Riding Education Committee), 34, 46, 52, 66, 69, 76, 77, 99, 113, 115-118
Walker, Arthur (monitor), 7
war emergency garden, 69, 70
War Loans, 42
War Savings Association, 41
War Wage, 45
Wayne University, Detroit, 77
Westfield Lane School, South Elmsall, 27, 42
Woolley Hall, 76

Zeppelins, 40-41